SCHOOL DAYS, COOL DAYS

Murray Paterson

Best wishes from
Murray Paterson

ISBN 978-0-557-05174-8

TABLE OF CONTENTS

ACKNOWLEDGEMENTS

I would like to thank several people, mostly teachers past and present, who supplied me with information that was necessary for the completion of this book. After being away from teaching for almost twenty-five years and with a memory that is not improving any, I needed, and appreciated, your help. Thank you all.

Special thanks are due also to my son Larry, grandson Joe, and friend Wally Henry for their assistance with the computer.

At the outset I should say that the names of people mentioned in this book have been changed.

PREFACE

This is a book that anyone who taught from the 1950s to the 1980s could have written. Sure, the classroom anecdotes would vary somewhat, but life in all schools back in those days followed very much a similar pattern over the years.

We taught in an era of several momentous changes, beginning with the baby boom when World War II ended in 1945. School enrolments sky-rocketed, schools were mushrooming up all across the nation, and teachers were very much in demand everywhere, a reversed situation from the 1930s when many teachers has a hard time getting a job. It was an age of consultants, when teachers with special skills and knowledge left the classroom to help other teachers in several areas of the curriculum, especially in large centres.

Within this time frame there were various improvements. Thanks to the economic postwar boom of the fifties and sixties teachers' salaries rose to a respective level in comparison with the rest of the work force, a far cry from the pittance they were in the great depression of the 1930s. New and improved audio-visual aids were having a positive impact on teaching procedures, along with the plethora of new textbooks in almost every subject on the curriculum.

At this time new developments took place in the educational scene. One-room rural schools were phased out and growing fleets of yellow buses could be seen arriving at both city and village schools with their precious cargos of school children. French became a new subject on the curriculum and it was the time when class trips, especially overnighters, became the in thing. There seemed to be no shortage of money for the advancement of education.

By the 1980s, however, circumstances in education were beginning to change. Enrolments started to decline, which led to a slow but sure process of closing some schools. As a result new teachers were once more finding it tougher to gain employment. Consultants in the system were being phased out and some of these people returned again to regular classroom teaching. The plentiful flow of money for school systems was easing up, and children even began knocking on doors frequently in school neighbourhoods selling goodies to raise money for class trips.

Also, various changes occurred in schools, some of which were both debatable and highly contested. The use of the Lord's Prayer disappeared from classrooms as did the strap, and the singing of religious Christmas carols, which had been enjoyed in schools for decades, was gradually phased out due to political correctness. The fear of violence and wrong-doing began to permeate the system as schools received bomb threats and were locked down until outside danger had been removed. From time to time parents in certain areas were concerned about reports of sexual deviators following children to and from school or offering them car rides. Life in the school environment had changed considerably in less than fifty years, and older people were now wondering what had happened to the more tranquil times they knew during their school years.

All these changes in this time period raise in my mind the question, were teachers of my generation teaching in the golden age of education?

PLAYGROUND MUSIC

One of the fondest memories of my elementary school teaching days was something that occurred not in the classroom but out in the schoolyard. I call it playground music. Perhaps you can recall it from your own childhood days.

It all begins when pupils arrive at school in the morning or are dismissed for recess. If you are near the schoolyard at first you hear a few pupils talking and can even make out parts of their conversations, but as more children appear on the scene there is a gradual buildup in volume and pitch as their talking increases. Finally it reaches the point where dozens of conflicting conversations drown out all the words and what remains is a constant babble of human voices. That's when playground music begins.

It is a rather unique sound, one that is difficult to describe. Basically it is light in quality and cheerful in tone, and if you are a short distance away from this children's concert it is next to impossible to distinguish any words coming from this playground melody. By way of comparison, imagine that you are eating some vegetable soup made from several vegetables which are finely chopped up and simmered for quite some time. You would find it difficult to distinguish the individual flavour of any one vegetable. So it is with this sound from the playground. The multitude of spoken words all blend together into an indistinguishable "schoolyard soup".

Sure, you'll hear the odd yelp, shriek, shout, and the occasional "bullfrog" voice of an adolescent grade 8 boy, but playground music consists mainly of a pleasant, youthful, treble-pitched sound that is delightful to listen to. About the only variation you hear in this music is the slight rising or falling in its volume from time to time. The closest comparison to it that I can think of is the sound of a large flock of Canada geese winging its way northward high in the sky singing away on a sunny April morning. Both the children and the geese produce a constant, happy, and vibrant sound.

Another interesting characteristic of playground music is that once it gets into full swing there are no moments of silence in it. It flows on continually just like a river. Wait as long as you like, you will find no pauses in this verbal action until the school bell rings to bring the pupils back into the classrooms.

You might think that playground music occurs only where there are large schools in urban centres, but such is not the case. I remember paddling a canoe about twenty years ago after my retirement up the Burnt River, a meandering stream ten to twenty miles north of the town of Lindsay, Ontario. I was on a stretch of water well treed on both sides and with no buildings in sight – quite a wild area, when I thought I could make out the sound of some children shouting in the distance. As I continued farther upstream the volume intensified as I drew nearer to its source. It sounded mighty like playground music to me, but away out here in the wilderness? So I took out my map to check my bearings, and sure enough, I was about half a mile away from the school in the nearby hamlet of Burnt River. I stopped paddling for a few minutes to listen to that pleasant   sound in a lovely, still setting. I suppose playground music is a universal song heard at schools of all sizes right across Canada.

Today I live close to an elementary school. A corner of my property abuts a corner of the school playground, so to this day I continue to hear and enjoy playground music. I should mention at this point that you can be too close to a schoolyard to hear the complete blending of children's voices. If you are right beside the pupils you can easily make out the conversations of the children nearest you. Often when I am working in the garden, raking leaves, shoveling snow, etc. I hear the bell ring to signal the start of recess. As I continue working I hear small groups of children's voices build up into playground music and I stop from time to time to listen carefully. It brings back fond memories not only of my teaching days but of my own days of attending an elementary school.

If you haven't been near a school for years I invite you to drive where you can park your car beside a school playground at recess, wind down the window, sit back, close your eyes, and enjoy some playground music. Perhaps it will help you recall some happy childhood memories.

THE INSPECTOR'S VISIT

I'm sure many of you will remember well from your elementary school days the inspector's annual visit. It usually began with a very formal greeting. After the inspector entered the classroom the teacher asked the pupils to stand. Then the inspector, beaming at the class from the front of the room, would say in a warm, friendly voice, "Good morning, girls and boys." And the class, having been well rehearsed for this occasion since early September would echo back in a singsong voice, "Good morning, Mr. Brown." After the pupils were seated the inspector usually did one of two things. He either retreated to a seat at the back of the room from which he observed the teacher in the course of his lessons, or he set about determining the pupils' progress in spelling, reading, arithmetic fundamentals, etc.

When he took over the class you likely thought, as a pupil, that he was inspecting you. My wife well remembers her inspector taking pupils out to the hall one at a time in her village school, and asking each pupil in turn to spell a few words orally. She says she shook in her shoes. When I was in grade 7 an inspector walked up and down the aisles observing us doing some seatwork. He stopped as he came by my desk and asked me to show him my Social Studies notebook. Oh oh, I thought, he's going to check my handwriting, my poorest subject. He merely flipped through a few pages quickly and then handed back the book without comment. I realized years later that he was likely checking up on subject content rather than the quality of my handwriting.

The main reason for the inspector's presence in your school was not to judge the class but to determine the teacher's effectiveness in his classroom. Naturally all teachers knew why the inspector was there, and did their best to make a good impression on him. Now stories abound about school inspectors' visits, and they often crop up as topics of conversation when retired teachers reminisce about the good old days in the classroom. With the passage of time it is difficult to verify whether such tales are fact or fiction, but some of them are just too good not to pass them on to you.

Apparently some teachers had their own special ploys to try to win brownie points with the inspector. One of the best known is the case of the teacher who prepared his class before the inspector's visit by telling them, "When Mr. Brown arrives for his annual visit I want you to do as follows: whenever I ask you a question all of you are to raise your hands to answer. If you think you know the right answer raise your right hand. If you are sure you don't know it raise your left hand. That way I'll know how to get the answers I want." I'm quite sure Mr. Brown, startled to see every hand go up after every question, would smell a rat right away.

A more subtle strategy was for the teacher to have ready what was known as a top drawer lesson. It was carefully planned out to be a super-duper, pull-out-all-the-stops masterpiece that would surely dazzle the inspector. Its presentation was thoroughly rehearsed, and then it was placed in the teacher's top desk drawer awaiting the inspector's visit. After the expected visitor arrived the teacher would finish the work at hand, then pull out his secret weapon, and with all the glitz, glitter, and glamour at his disposal fire it off on his pupils. This seemed like a stunt that might work.

On the other hand the inspectors were not without their own bags of tricks. One of them visited me during the last hour of the school day, strangely enough. He observed me teaching a history lesson and just after I had assigned the class their seatwork he came up to my desk at the front of the room. After he began a conversation he started to execute a well-planned dance. Picking up my seating plan from the desk and talking all the while he sidled over to the blackboard, turned towards the class, and planted his hips firmly against the blackboard ledge. I, as his dancing partner, was obliged to pirouette 180 degrees with my back to the class in order to face him. He must have conversed for five to ten minutes, mostly about nothing in particular. During this time he continually glanced at the seating plan, picked out a name, then looked around me to see what that certain pupil was doing. I knew what he was up to. He was not interested in the pupils' names but merely wanted an excuse to observe them in action while the class knew I couldn't see what was going on behind my back. From the look on his face nothing amiss seemed to be happening. I had faith that my class would not let me down. After this brief encounter he bid me adieu and left.

It was always an advantage to have advance knowledge of an inspector's presence in the school. That way as a teacher you had a few moments to gain your composure and set the proper tone for the class to receive this important visitor. If you could see him parking his car at the school parking lot so much the better. I heard of one teacher who was in this envied position in a village school with just a few classrooms. Whenever she saw the inspector's car drive up she reached for a ready-made note in her desk, handed it to a reliable pupil, and told her to deliver it to the other teachers. It read, "Who has the blue-handled scissors?" Talk about the jungle drums beating! I was told that one day the inspector intercepted the delivery girl and read the note. I'm quite sure he read between the lines on that one.

Finally, here is how two young teachers fell out of favour with their inspectors. Harry was a very slow individual – slow to move, slow to speak, slow in doing everything. One morning he was driving his car to teach at his one-room rural school and he was a few minutes late. That was no problem for Harry, but as he neared the school he noticed that there were no children on the playground, "That's odd," thought Harry. "I don't think today is Saturday." Then he noticed a car parked beside the school. Something strange was going on here, and as he opened the school door he got the answer to his riddle. There before him were all his pupils properly seated at their desks, and at his desk sat the inspector. What a way to start a school day!

George also taught in a one-room rural school, but in a different inspectorate. One afternoon during the last week of June his inspector dropped by to see him. When he opened the door he found nobody there. So he went to the nearest house and asked a lady how come no one was at the school. "Oh," she said, "George and the kids are all down at the lake swimming at the sandy beach. They're doing that every afternoon this week." There is nothing like a long class party to end the school year. Fortunately for George he had earlier handed in his resignation at that school and was headed for a different inspectorate in September.

PERSONALITY TYPES

Here's a chapter that all teachers with a few years experience can easily relate to – the wide differences in personality types that are evident in a classroom. Even if you were not a teacher I'm sure you will recall having classmates like some of the following in your years at school.

Teacher's Pet

Jean was a very well liked young lady, and it was no wonder. She was always calm, serene, contented, and co-operative. I can't ever recall her being angry, let alone being annoyed about anything. She never complained or bad-mouthed anyone. These qualities account for the fact that she was always cheerful. I remember one afternoon when the class had left for the day, Jean and the other blackboard monitor were erasing the work on the boards, and all the while she was humming softly. Is it any wonder that I had a problem trying not to favour her? If all the pupils in your class were like Jean you would think you had died and were in heaven.

The Silent One

If as a supply teacher you taught the class Bill was in, even after a week you probably wouldn't realize he was there. While he could speak, he did so very rarely that you would think he was tongue-tied. Bill was simply one of those individuals who just don't care to talk. I found him to be an average pupil academically, and he got along with his peers quite well, but he just did not want to talk. In an attempt to find out why he was so uncommunicative I detained him momentarily after school one day and asked him why he never volunteered to answer any questions I asked the class. After a short pause he stated that he was fearful of giving wrong answers. I let him go and pondered about what he said. I did not believe him, for whenever I asked him his fair share of my questions he usually came up with the right answers. By his statement he was simply putting me off and so I let the matter drop. Twice since my retirement I have met Bill and had a pleasant chat with him. He now seems more willing to converse. Could it be that his wife solved his problem?

The Talker

If Bill was the quiet one then Melissa was his opposite. She enjoyed talking, or I should say she liked to hear conversation going on around her as much as possible. When we were in a question and answer mode she seemed quite content, but when the class was quietly working at some seatwork assignment that was another story. She overcame these periods of silence in two ways, both of which you might label artificial talking. From time to time any boss will look out at his workers just to see how things are going, and teachers do likewise with their pupils. Sometimes when I looked at Melissa I noticed her lips moving. Obviously she was verbalizing words connected with the work on her desk.

Melissa usually finished her assigned work well before other pupils. (She did everything quickly.) When I walked up and down the aisles to see how far along everyone was in completing their work I would see Melissa writing herself notes in her workbook. Again, this was another attempt on her part to produce "silent talking". Perhaps she had this oddity in her personality because she was a rather high-strung individual and found oral language to be a way to relieve tension.

Temper Tantrum Tony

Tony's problem was that he was extremely quick-tempered. If there were pupils engaged in some kind of scuffle out on the playground it would be a fairly safe bet that Tony would be right in the middle of it, with either his mouth or his fists going full tilt. After a teacher intervened, separated Tony and his opponent, and then tried to find out the cause of the ruckus, it was usually a misunderstanding or some trivial matter. Tony's line of rationalizing seemed to be, if I can put you down either verbally with my mouth or physically with my fists then I must be right.

The strange thing was that when he was not in a fighting mood he was a rather calm and reserved individual. This gave him a certain Jekyll and Hyde complex. He reminded me of a well-known defenceman on the Maple Leafs' team who was apparently a gentleman off the ice but an infamous ruffian once he put his skates on. My hope for Tony was that he would get over his fits of temper before his body matured and he got out into the world of work.

A Disguised Genius

There was a time in our school system when all grade 8 pupils were given an annual I.Q. (intelligence quotient) test. It was always interesting to match a pupil's academic achievement i.e., report card marks with his/her I.Q. score to see how they compared. We had one young lady named Sally who proved to be an interesting case. She did very well in all her school subjects but her I.Q. was right on 100, which indicates the intelligence of an average individual. Thinking that something was amiss the principal had her tested anew. Again she came up with that average score of 100. This had me wondering, was she overachieving in her school work or did she have some phobia about I.Q. tests? She continued to do well up to the time she graduated from grade 8, and I did not think any more about it at the time.

About twenty years later I was walking down the halls of a local public high school when I noticed a framed list of years and names of students. It contained the names of the boy and girl who were voted the best all-round students each year by their peers. I was delighted to see Sally's name on that list.

Look Out World, Here I Come

Unfortunately we have from time to time in the classroom a person like Annie whose main interest in life seems to be flaunting himself or herself whenever possible. You could readily pick her out in the class photo. She was the one wearing not ordinary clothing like the others, but a loud, garish getup you might expect to see at a costume party. When it came to volunteering to do some project, Annie would be the first with her hand in the air, despite her lack of talent in many areas. She wanted to be friends with everyone but was shunned by many because of her strange behaviour. Although she was a difficult pupil to teach I felt sorry for her because she seemed unaware of the fact that she was crying for attention.

I met Annie downtown several years later where she had two children with her. We had a pleasant talk, from which I gathered that her life had become more settled than when I taught her. No doubt having a family had something to do with that.

Mr. or Miss Everything

At the opposite end of the spectrum from Annie was Fred. About once every decade I had a pupil like Fred, who seemed to excel at everything he turned his hand to. Though not the top scholar in the class he was well up there. Fred's athletic prowess was outstanding – on school teams, at field day events, and of course in Physical Education classes. He was an excellent singer and his artwork was a joy to behold. In all phases of his school work he did his best, and despite his many favourable attributes he remained a rather modest person and was well liked by all. Fred was the kind of pupil a teacher remembers over his lifetime.

When a teacher inherits a new class each September it is something like putting a jigsaw puzzle together. With the latter it is a matter of taking all those physical shapes and coloured pieces and assembling them together into a pretty picture. With the former it is a matter of taking a wide variety of personalities and somehow blending them together to form a workable unit in this task of learning a prescribed curriculum over the ensuing year.

GOOD CLASSES, BAD CLASSES

If you were never in the teaching profession you probably thought that when you were in elementary school all classes were pretty much the same. To you a typical class might have contained an Einstein (the brain of the class), a pretty girl known as Miss Canada, a handsome boy nicknamed Romeo, a Tom Sawyer type who was averse to learning schoolwork, the tough guy who always carried a chip on his shoulder, the ubiquitous class clown, and of course one or two teacher's pets. All your other classmates were likely considered to be average people. If you attended a fairly small school you probably moved from grade to grade with the same classmates, so that you would not have been in a position to compare your class to other ones. Also, at that tender age you likely did not discern human characteristics the way you did when you moved on to high school, and were more apt to have different classmates in your room each succeeding year.

On the other hand teachers know very well that all classes are not the same, and after teaching only a few years they discover that there are good classes and there are bad classes. In my experience I found that roughly every seven years I was teaching a superb class and somewhere in between those seven years I had the misfortune of winding up with a group of cantankerous pupils. As you might expect during the other years I found myself teaching average, run-of-the-mill classes.

So my career was like riding a roller-coaster; sometimes I seemed to be on top of the world, everything went smoothly, and the time seemed to fly by pleasantly. Then, before I knew it, I found myself in the depths of despondency and couldn't wait till the end of June came along when I could hope for a better group of pupils the next year. Like a lot of situations in life I did not realize or appreciate at the time that with a good class I had such a pleasant group of young people to work with. Then all of a sudden I was brought back to reality when I had a group before me who were more bent on mischief than learning. It was like having a delightful dream changing into a nightmare.

In the later years of my career I felt sorry when I observed a first year teacher who had the misfortune of being in charge of a group of trouble-makers and had no experience as to how to handle them. I remember telling such tyros to grin and bear it, that there was a silver lining at the end of their grey cloud, and that next year things would be better. When you're down the only way is up. At this point I must tell you about a young lady who graduated from normal school and began her career in a primary class in the downtown core of a large city. When she upbraided one little fellow for his misbehaviour he shot back, "When my brother gets out of jail he'll fix you!"

By now you're probably wondering what makes a class "good or bad". A desirable class isn't necessarily one that has a preponderance of scholars, although it is certainly helpful if pupils are willing to learn. A good class is one where the pupils exemplify getalongability, to use a home made word. They conform to class routines readily, are thoughtful and helpful to others, and want to do the right thing. In short they are a positive and cohesive unit. When I was transferred one year to a new school different staff members told me that I was getting a superb class, and they were right. They had seen this group of pupils advancing year by year through the grades and knew what a good class it was. In my thirty-five years of teaching it was one of my best classes.

On the other hand a bad class is made up largely of individuals who are just that – individuals, not team players.

They are self-centred, self-seeking miscreants whose goal in school is not to extend the common good but to gain attention by means of disruptive behaviour.

A good example of this was Tim, a good-looking, well built and well dressed grade 8 boy with an arrogant manner. In the same room was Tom, a poor, soft-spoken lad who, like the weak chicken in the flock was picked on by the more able classmates around him. Apparently Tim picked a fight with Tom on their way home from school one afternoon. "Easy pickings," Tim probably thought. Well, next morning before 9:00 A. M. two other boys told me about the fight. Tom had easily beaten Tim, They said, "Tom really cleaned his clock." I said nothing about it to anyone but thought to myself that Tim got what he deserved.

You don't have to teach a particular group of pupils to know if things are going well with them or not. If you have been in a school for only a few years you can form an opinion of them both by observing them around the school and by their reputation. This is especially true of an unco-operative class. I remember watching a rowdy class of youngsters while on playground duty over the years. One recess during the April before I was going to "inherit" them I couldn't miss the chance. While the main ringleaders were together in one part of the playground I forewarned them, "You folks had better straighten up before you get to my room next September." By the looks on their faces I could tell that they knew exactly what I meant. I had a reputation for brooking no nonsense.

In a different school the longtime caretaker observed another wild group coming up through the grades. I had them early in my career in a grade 7 class. On the first school day the next September he came into my room after dismissal for the day and said to me, totally unannounced, "I've been waiting for this day for the last seven years. Maybe Mr. Fee (the principal who was to teach them in their grade 8 year) will finally straighten them out." Both men knew this class all too well.

There is one thing that good and bad classes have in common; they both have ringleaders who either help or hinder the teacher in setting the tone of the classroom. The other class members, perhaps unknowingly, look up to these key people and follow their lead in the setting of the atmosphere that pervades every classroom. As one inspector said to me, "If a classroom door is open I can walk slowly down the hall and immediately sense the tone of the class within that room."

WHAT! THE TEACHER WAS LATE?

During my teaching career I prided myself on two accomplishments. In thirty-five years I missed a total of only fifty-six days off the job. These included some half days for funerals, single days for writing university exams, and anywhere from one to three days due to illnesses some years, mostly common colds picked up between November and March. As one doctor told me, "How can teachers possibly avoid getting colds with all those children coughing and sneezing around them five hours a day?"

Also, I was never late for school. Well, hardly ever – twice to be honest with you, and both times it was not my fault. (For the other occasion see chapter 14 for the interesting circumstances that caused my tardiness that time.)

The school where I began my teaching, Lakefield Public School, was in the inspectorate of Mr. Barker. His sphere of operations was quite large as it included over half of Peterborough County, and this meant that he spent a lot of time on the road driving from school to school. In the early 1950s he came up with a great idea. When enough educational matters arose to make it worthwhile he called a meeting for the staffs of his three largest schools, those in Norwood, Havelock, and

Lakefield. They were to meet in one of the villages during the latter part of a Friday afternoon. The pupils, with advanced notice sent to their parents, were dismissed early. (There was no need to worry about changing bus schedules as all elementary school pupils walked to school in those days.) The meeting consisted of two parts. First Mr. Barker informed us of the latest news in the world of education and he also told us of any new policy or changes he was putting into effect. This was followed by a social time of "tea and crumpets" served by the ladies of the host school.

This new venture was quite successful for various reasons. It saved the inspector time in traveling and talking, he could use this larger audience (about twenty teachers) as a sounding board on which to bounce off new ideas, the pupils enjoyed an earlier start to the weekend, and the teachers from different schools could share their ideas informally in "mini-grade" meetings over a cup of tea and a sandwich.

Now to get on to why I was late. While there was no apparent rivalry among the three groups of ladies serving the food, each naturally wanted to put on a good show when it became their turn to act as hostesses. One of our staff knew an elderly widow in town named Bertha Kennedy, who owned a lovely silver tea service. After she got Bertha's consent to borrow it I was asked if I would drive it to school on the Friday afternoon of our meeting since I lived quite close to her. Agreeing readily, I figured ten minutes would be ample time to pick it up and drive to school before bell time. School law required teachers to be at their schools at least five minutes before afternoon assembly. I was in for a bit of a shock.

Although I had seen Bertha and waved to her in passing several times I had never conversed with her before so I really didn't know her. I expected that she would have her tea service ready for me, and after a quick thank you I would be on my way. Far from it. When I rapped on her door she greeted me like a long-lost friend, asked me to sit down (a mistake on my part), and then went scurrying to a back room to get the tea service. All the while she carried on a nonstop conversation about affairs in the village and when she returned she insisted that I have a cup of tea. I stated emphatically that I had to get to school right away. It was as though she never heard me. As she prattled on effortlessly I began to worry about the time. Even looking directly at my watch had no effect on her. She simply had no concern about the passage of time.

Finally I had had enough of this. I stood up, grabbed the tea service, thanked Bertha profusely, and hurried to my car. As I raced to the school in my old flivver I was thankful that the local policeman hadn't seen me in what must have been a record trip to work. But as I neared the school and saw the empty playground I realized I was late.

My plan now was to sneak quickly and quietly into the school unnoticed, drop off the tea service at the office, and then proceed unruffled to my classroom. This was not to be. Even before I got out of the car I looked up at my classroom windows on the second floor of the school. There stood three of the braver types in the class looking down at me, awaiting my presence and wondering no doubt why I was late getting to school. By the time I started walking up the sidewalk towards the building these three had called their classmates to come to the windows to see an unusual spectacle. Here was my entire class smiling and giggling as they watched their teacher enter the school carrying a silver tea service. Talk about an embarrassing situation!

I realized I had some explaining to do to my pupils or they would embellish this incident away out of proportion at their homes that evening. So I leveled with them. I was concise, but I did not mention Bertha Kennedy's name. After all, in such a small community she might be the grandmother of one of my pupils. I said something to the effect that I had been asked to bring the tea service to school for use at the afternoon teachers' meeting and that I was unavoidably delayed in procuring it. I trusted that this explanation would satisfy their curiosity.

The meeting went well and so did the tea, during which I listened carefully expecting to overhear favourable comments about the silver tea service. Although I heard none I hoped that they liked it, especially after all the trouble I went through to get it. I also hoped that none of my pupils' parents would ask that old perennial standby at the supper table that evening, "What happened at school today?"

MAY I LEAVE THE ROOM?

I'm sure you all remember that question being asked many times over during your early years at school. The answer the teacher gave was very likely yes. If for some reason the teacher said no there might have been dire consequences. I could tell you some I've heard of and they are quite gruesome, but I don't think that is proper or necessary at this time. I realize that this topic is a rather touchy one.

As I see it there were three misdemeanours that sometimes happened when the teacher answered yes to the above question. The first was that it could become a game in some classes. If the teacher automatically and quickly said yes without giving the matter any thought the pupils would soon learn that here was a very easy route to get away from a dull, boring lesson, have a chance to enjoy some exercise by stretching their legs, or simply get a change of scenery. What the teacher should have done is to pause for a moment, give the pupil that "teacher's look" which only teachers can give, and then say yes. I really think some teachers, even though they knew these pupils were playing a mean game, would rather go along with it than suffer parental repercussions by trying to clamp down on a perennial parade to the washroom.

It's hard to imagine that the next situation really happened but it did, as some people involved in this misdeed have told me. It started out with Johnny's asking to leave the room, to which the teacher replied yes. Then, within the next half minute, Billy suddenly decided he had to go, and likewise asked for permission to go to the washroom. And, would you believe it, the teacher actually let him walk out of the room then and there! Now Billy's bladder was not causing him any trouble. The truth is he just wanted to join his friend Johnny for a little free time from the classroom. I find it hard to believe that some teachers did not smell a rat in this scenario. The teacher's obvious answer to Billy's request should have been, "Yes, you may, as soon as Johnny gets back."

The third mishap was more serious. I know of some cases where damage was done to school property by pupils on their way to or from the washroom. The culprits of these deeds may have had their evil intent pre-planned and just used the familiar washroom question as a means of getting to the scene of their crimes, or with time on their hands on their round trip to the toilet it may have been a matter of the devil makes idle hands busy. The motive for their mischief was irrelevant. Damage was done and the offenders needed to be found out and punished.

After one of these incidents a principal called all the boys from grade 4 to 8 to the General Purpose Room and gave them quite a blasting. It neither divulged the guilty boy nor stopped further damage from being done so he tried something else. He asked those teachers concerned to keep a record for a week of the names of pupils who asked to go to the washroom and the time of day they went.

After the week was up he called a meeting of the grade 4 to 8 teachers and without mentioning any names he gave us some interesting information. He told us the number of pupils in each class who left the room during the week. Three classes had what

I thought were abnormally high numbers. He also said that there were two cases where two pupils were out of the room at the same time. Now telling us these facts may not have led to finding the guilty party right off, but indirectly it may have had a beneficial result. I think the only reason he gave us these numbers was to give some teachers a message, namely that if some teachers had only a few pupils leave the room during a week perhaps others could work on cutting back on their high numbers.

I heard of one teacher who had a unique way of handling this business of pupils leaving the room. She told her pupils to hold up their hands in a certain position which meant they needed to go to the washroom. In this way the teacher could simply look at the pupil, give him a nod, and away he went. This would work beautifully during a question and answer session as the lesson would progress without that usual, well-known verbal interruption.

Personally I had almost no difficulty with this matter of leaving the room as I instituted an honour system in the very early years of my career. I did this for two reasons. First, by the look on their faces I could tell that some pupils found it embarrassing to ask the age-old question. Secondly, rather than ask it some pupils preferred to fidget in their seats and wait for the dismissal bell to ring. I could tell by this unusual action that they had more than ants in their pants.

So at the start of the year I told the class that they did not need to ask permission to leave the room. They were to get up quietly and leave. (I also told them that any time they felt sick they were to get out of the room as fast as they could go!) Now you might think that with this carte blanche there would be a continuous procession to the washroom all day, but such was not the case. They responded to the fact that I had leveled with them, and over the course of a year they rarely left the room.

There was one exception to this procedure, however. His

name was Bob. Now Bob was not a well boy. He often appeared tired, had a pale complexion, and seemed to be in a daze much of the time. Although he left the room more than the rest of the class put together I don't honestly think he was taking advantage of our honour system. I really think the poor lad had kidney problems.

We were all working away quietly at our desks one late afternoon just a few minutes before dismissal time. Bob stood up and headed for the door. As he got there I asked, "Where are you going?" What a stupid question to ask! I knew where he was going. What I implied by my question was that since it was nearly time to go home could he wait until the bell rang. He gave me a very forthright answer. "I'm going for a leak." With that I quickly waved my arm to the door, so much as to say, "Get out of here!" I learned something that day – I must work on improving my questioning skills.

ORDERLY DESKS

In my third year of teaching I came up with an idea for a new class routine, although the origin of it was unusual. One winter morning shortly before 9:00 A.M. I walked across the hall to the principal's classroom (a full time teaching one) to see him about some matter. As I passed through his open door I could not see him at first, and then I noticed him squatting down beside a pupil's desk. He was busy pulling out handful after handful of materials from that desk and simply letting them fall to the floor in a jumbled pile. What a mess he was extracting – dog-eared notebooks, an assortment of writing tools, scrambled textbooks, candy wrappers, you name it!

It wasn't an easy chore he had as much of this mess was well jammed together in a rather small area. He had his back to me, and as he was so intent on this unusual occupation he didn't know I was just a short distance behind him. I thought to myself that at this time he would be in no mood to talk with me about anything so I quietly backed away and returned to my room. No doubt some untidy pupil got the shock of his life as he neared his desk that morning and the class probably received a lecture on keeping their desks tidy.

I thought about this untidy desk during that day, and at recess I checked the condition of a few desks in my classroom. They were not too bad but some could have been better. Then I arrived at the idea of having the pupils keep all their books in the same order all the time. Now you may think that this was too much regimentation, but let me tell you how it worked and what its benefits were.

All the notebooks were put into one pile and all the textbooks into another one. At the end of the school day rulers, pencils, pens, and erasers were placed between the two piles of neatly stacked books, ready to be taken out quickly first thing after the class sat down next morning. Notebooks were arranged with those used most often near the top of the pile and those used less often near the bottom. As I recall it now the order went something like this: workbook, Arithmetic, Spelling, Composition, Grammar, Social Studies, and Science. With the textbooks we had the largest one at the bottom of the pile and successively smaller ones placed on top. Textbooks used less often e.g., music books, were kept at the front or back of the room on shelves. This was the total contents inside the desk – no gum, candy, comic books, and the like.

Now how did this system work? Let's say I told the class to take out their Spelling notebooks. Each pupil began counting down mentally in the notebook pile "1, 2", lift them up a little, and then slide out the third book down. When it was placed on the desk tops the name on all the books would be Spelling. To return the book to its rightful place they repeated the 1, 2 count and slid it back into place. It was as simple as that. Using this system saved time, fuss, dog-eared books, and established two desirable habits – neatness and organization.

Now how much time did this method save? Imagine if this system wasn't in use and the teacher asked the class to take out their readers. Do you remember someone in one of your classrooms (there was always at least one) who forever was the last to get a book out of the desk? He/she would fuss and fiddle, pull out the wrong book, drop one or two others on the floor, grope around doubled over into the desk again and finally get the desired book to the desktop. This ungainly process wasted about a minute of class time. I think it's safe to assume that a pupil took out and replaced books an average of seven times a day. Multiply that by 190 school days a year (no P.A. days or snow days back then!) and you get 1330 minutes. Divide that by sixty and you end up with just over twenty-two hours – almost a full day lost, evaporated into thin air. Pupils were always amazed when I worked out these numbers for them on the blackboard the first school day in September.

So we would practise this routine the first week of each school year. They appreciated how quick and easy it was to do, but probably weren't aware that their books remained in better condition thanks to this method. What they did not realize, and what I hoped would come true, was that they were learning two good habits that just might carry over into their adult lives, namely tidiness and orderliness. As one principal once said to his staff, "School may be the only place where some children learn law and order."

BEAN BAG ARITHMETIC

Here's an oral number facts drill I picked up from a fellow teacher well on down the road in my teaching career. I called it bean bag arithmetic because it involved two subjects, physical education and arithmetic. A rather unusual combination, wouldn't you say?

This is how it went. I stood at the front of the classroom with a bean bag in my hand, called out a multiplication combination e.g., "7 x 6" and then threw the bag towards a pupil. The object of the game was that he or she was to say the right answer "42" before catching the bag. Then the pupil threw it back to me. If the answer given was correct I threw the bag to another pupil. If it was wrong I said the right answer as the bag returned to me.

The first time each year I played this game with a new class there were a few wrinkles to be ironed out. The first was that some eager beavers would reach an arm high overhead and intercept the bean bag. I'm sure they did not mean any harm by doing this. They were just caught up in the excitement of the action and it was quite excusable. And let's face it, if I didn't throw it accurately it was difficult for the class to know just who was supposed to catch that thing. Over time this situation improved as my aim got better and they became more used to the game.

The opposite reaction was when some people saw the bag coming towards them and decided to solve the problem by dodging the toss. By doing this they hoped to put the onus of catching the bag on the person seated behind them. There was no excuse for this, and any offenders soon knew it. Some time in the next three or four tosses they would find the bag coming at them again. It didn't take them long to figure out that it would be better for them on the next day we had this drill to make an honest attempt at giving an answer and trying to catch the bag the first time it came their way. Another way to foil the bag dodgers was to have all pupils in a row move their chairs a little in a zigzag pattern down the row. Now there was no doubt as to who should catch the bag.

The teacher's immediate aim of this drill of course was to have each pupil give a correct answer before catching the bean bag. But as I told the class I expected that everyone would try to say the right answer mentally before the person selected said it aloud. To achieve this end I tried a number of devices to keep them guessing as to where I was going to throw the bag. One way was to look to the left but throw it to someone still within my vision to the right. Or raise my head up a bit, look at the pupils at the back of the room, and then plop it to someone right in front of me. Those who sat in the front corner of the room to my left might have felt that they were more or less out of the line of the general flow of traffic. To keep them attentive I would occasionally look to my right, say a combination, then suddenly toss the bag in a backhand throw around behind my back. Yet another feint was to hold the bag in my left hand, say a combination, toss the bag over to my right hand, and then quickly throw it out in a leftward direction. All of these tricks kept the class on their toes.

To say that I threw the bag at my pupils is not an accurate statement. I did not hurl or fling a missile at them, but rather I lobbed or tossed a soft object in their direction. The bag was always thrown underhand and usually made a gentle arc upwards in its progression from teacher to pupil. Since those nearest to me had less time to react when the bag was tossed I usually lobbed it more gently and made the bag pass through a slightly higher arc than tosses made to those near the back of the room. For really bright pupils near the back seats I sometimes threw the bag faster, or put less arc in it, or did not say the combination until the bag was actually sailing through the air. These keener pupils really enjoyed the challenge.

Before we began the first trial run of this drill each year I stressed with the class not to worry about the physical education part of this exercise. I said don't be concerned about catching the bag, but try to say the answer before the bag lands on your desk. Despite this encouragement there were usually a few pupils who just did not like this activity. It may have been a lack of knowing the multiplication tables on their part, the fear of the bean bag coming at them like, in their minds, an aerial juggernaut, or the fact that they felt they were being put on the spot in front of their classmates. It was most rewarding to me, however, to see some of these pupils improve over the year in this discipline. I hoped that it would inspire them to work at improving their number facts.

In a year when I had a class that was up to the mark in arithmetic it was a real joy for me to go through this bean bag routine with them. We could keep the bag moving at a good clip with very few wrong answers being given. As the year progressed my tossing aim improved as did their return throw. We developed a smooth rhythm to it both physically and arithmetically. I could get around to the whole class in a matter of just a few minutes.

In all honesty I must admit that I'm glad this bean bag game was not in vogue when I was a pupil in the senior grades of elementary school. The physical education part of it I would have relished but arithmetic was not my strong subject.

WINTER FUN?

I suppose most adults would agree that winter is not their favourite time of the year, what with the shorter daylight hours, cold temperatures, treacherous ice underfoot, shoveling sidewalks and driveways, and extra expenses with more fuel and electricity used. But let's face it, kids love winter and have a great deal of fun playing with ice and snow.

Do you remember some of these winter activities on the school playground? The first of these probably occurred in November when enough packy snow allowed you to practise your aim in throwing snowballs. Or perhaps you got involved in a contest to see who could roll the biggest snowball, sometimes making them so large that it took   two or three of you just to roll it along as it grew nearly as big as you. Maybe you lay on your back in some deep fluffy snow, swung your arms and legs sideways back and forth a few times, and then stood up to admire the snow angels you had made. When conditions were right you likely took a run and slid time and again across a sheet of shiny new ice, or better still you may have coasted on the seat of your britches down a hill, if you were lucky enough to have one at your school. Then you could always make snowmen or snowforts if the snow was of the right consistency. Usually neither of these had a very long life on a school playground. Finally, when winter was well under way you may have been fortunate enough to have an interested teacher and his grade 8 class make and maintain a skating rink on school premises. As well as using it to good advantage during Physical Education periods it also provided entertainment after dismissal time and before the onset of darkness.

All of these pastimes are enjoyed by children but two of them can be a cause of concern for school administration, namely sliding and snowballing. Sliding across flat terrain doesn't present much of a problem but scooting down a slope, especially a steep one, can lead to injuries. The risk is increased when some pupils slide into others at the bottom of the run.

At one school we had a gentle gradient on part of the playground, and the slides thereon would not likely have led to any accidents except for one factor – Willie. Now Willie was one of those unfortunate children who might best be described as an accident waiting for a place to happen. That place was on one of those innocent-looking slides. If anyone in the school was going to be injured in some freakish way you could bet your bottom dollar that person would be Willie. It seems that one morning before 9:00 A.M. the children were enjoying an early morning slide when it happened. Someone bumped into Willie at the end of one slide and his leg was broken.

After this unfortunate accident the principal's dilemma was whether to allow the pupils to continue having their fun sliding on this slope or to prevent further injury ban the use of these slides. So he called a staff meeting to get our opinion on this matter. Two ladies on the staff who were quite the nervous Nellys insisted that there should be no further sliding on school property, not even on level terrain. They claimed it was just too dangerous. Immediately I balked at this idea, stating that with Willie now unable to use the slides it was highly unlikely that any other child in the school would be injured coasting down such a gentle gradient. You might guess the outcome of this perplexity. Can you stop a bird from flying, or a fish from swimming, or young children from sliding down an icy slope?

Throwing snowballs also presented a problem at some schools. If you were ever hit in the face by a hard-packed, granular snow missile you'll know exactly what I mean. In my experience snowballing policy was set by each individual school and varied from don't throw any snowballs at all (under the penalty of receiving the strap) all the way to you may throw them when and wherever you like.

One principal set the tone re snowballing for his school quite succinctly just before one November morning recess bell. Over the public address system he announced in rather poetic fashion, "Snow is falling softly to the ground." Then after a short pause he barked out in a military tone, "Leave it there!" In another school the principal went one step further. He not only banned snowballing on school property but attempted to stop it on the pupils' walk to and from school. I imagine in the area beyond sight of the school this would have been as enforceable as requiring birds not to sing.

At the other end of the scale were schools where there was no snowballing policy; just throw them where you will. Now you might think that this would be courting disaster, but in schools where I taught that had this course of action I don't recall things getting out of hand. Sure, there were the occasional snowball battles, with two large armies of boys trying to drive each other backwards into submission but at no time do I remember these fellows pelting school property or throwing snow at the fairer sex. If they had I'm sure they would have been dealt with promptly. With the beginning of each new winter at these schools the pupils seemed to remember what was right and wrong when it came to throwing snowballs and acted accordingly.

In one school we had an intermediate step between these two extremes. The layout of the playground at this school provided a natural area for snowballing with easily recognized boundaries. If you wanted to throw snowballs you did so only in this site. If you didn't want this annoyance you stayed out of the area, which soon became known as no-man's-land. This system was very successful as it pleased both the warriors and the pacifists.

So while most of us no longer relish winter as we get older perhaps this chapter will bring back some happy memories of winter days you had at school.

CAN I GET A TEACHING JOB?

It's strange how two decades could bring about such a complete change in the teachers' job market, but it happened between 1930 and 1950. It was caused by two horrendous events in world history, namely the great depression of the 1930s and World War II (1939-1945).

When the stock markets crashed in October 1929 the economy throughout the developed world went into a tailspin. Times were tough. For some people it was a struggle to get enough food for regular meals. One of my pre-school memories is that of a man walking down our street and rapping at one door after another. Finally at one house he was in luck. After a brief conversation with the lady of the house she came back to the door and handed the man a knife, fork, and plate of food. He then sat on the verandah steps and ate his meal using his lap for a table. That's how hard pressed some people were to get their daily bread.

Jobs were tough to come by also, and this was especially true for young people starting out into the world of work, as beginning teachers of that era well knew. Before commencing a career in a city school it was well understood that an apprenticeship came first in one of the many one-room rural schools throughout Ontario. Job openings were so few and far between that some graduates from normal schools (later known as teachers' colleges) did not get teaching jobs and had to go into some other line of work. One lady told me that she did not acquire a teaching position after her graduation in 1934 till July 15. The three men rural school boards of that era were well aware of the plight of beginning teachers and, money being the scarce commodity that it was, were able to get away with paying tyros a mere pittance. I was told by people who began teaching back in those days that in our part of the country a yearly salary of $400 to $600 was considered to be quite an acceptable sum. I also heard of graduates underbidding one another in an attempt to get a teaching job. There was no unemployment insurance or welfare back then, and the song that best summed up that era was Brother, Can You Spare a Dime? No wonder that decade was referred to as the dirty thirties.

With the war starting in September, 1939 job opportunities for teachers changed for the better, slowly at first and then dramatically as the war got into full swing. This was obviously due to the fact that a number of teachers put their careers on hold while they volunteered to join the armed forces. As an interesting aside, so many men working in factories left to go to war that plants converting to production for military purposes were obliged to hire women to replace them to make goods for the war effort. This movement was well expressed in the song Rosie, the Riveter. It was during the war that the change took place from married women being full-time housewives to both adults working beyond the home.

This change occurred for teachers also during the war. To the best of my knowledge it was 1943 when the first married lady was hired as a teacher by our board of education. Up till that time all lady teachers were single women, and if any of them decided to get married they were obliged to give up teaching. I well remember that happening in the elementary school I attended.

At the end of the war a new era in Canada began, aptly named the baby boom. What with all those servicemen returning home it wasn't long before Canada's population increased considerably. By the 1950s decade baby boomers were off to classes enlarging the country's school population to unprecedented numbers. It very soon became a problem of where to put them all, and four solutions followed. First of all those schools that had unused basement rooms that could be converted to classrooms had a ready answer to the problem. While the occupants of these rooms may have felt somewhat claustrophobic they had one great advantage. Since these rooms were at least partly under ground level they would have been warmer in winter and cooler in May, June, and September.

If a schoolyard had sufficient acreage another common adaptation was to build an addition on to the original school building. In many schools this is when they first had facilities such as libraries and general purpose rooms, which were incorporated into the new structure.

A new trend started in the 1950s. One or more prefabricated classrooms were moved on to the school property, readily adjacent to an outside door of the main building. In this way children had handy access to the facilities in the larger school structure. Portables, as they were called, were cheaper to erect than adding on an addition directly to the school. Another advantage of bringing in portables was that if for some reason there was a significant decline in enrolment at their present location they could be moved to another site that needed more classrooms. This was a considerable part of one house-moving company's operations in central southern Ontario back then.

With the economic boom of the 1950s and 1960s cities and towns were mushrooming at a prodigious rate, expanding outward into their suburban areas. These of course had to be serviced by new schools and they were built at an astounding rate. I read years ago that across Canada, for some time period which I have forgotten (but obviously one found within these two decades), a new school was constructed and ready for use on an average of one school every day! When I tallied all the schools that I knew of in Peterborough County that were built in this time frame, thirty in all, that figure of one school a day doesn't surprise me in the least.

And how did all this affect the matter of teachers getting jobs? That's not hard to guess. When it came to getting the teaching position they would like to have, teachers never had it so good, and probably never will again. If a teacher with experience desired a change of location, whether it was to leave an undesirable situation at his/her present school or to go to another venue with something better to offer there were many openings with the local boards of education in cities. Or if a teacher wished to live and teach in another part of the province that too was no obstacle, for the Toronto newspapers had column after column in their want ads sections devoted to job opportunities for teachers all across the province.

These years were also a time when a number of new positions beyond the classroom became available in elementary schools. In 1950 an average sized school board may have had one music supervisor and that was it. Fifteen to twenty years later that same board probably had a wide variety of supervisors, consultants, and counselors – art, French, audio-visual aids, physical education, outdoor education, primary methods, and guidance, to name a few. A number of teachers left their classrooms to fill these positions, wherein they had special knowledge, skills, and interests.

Now, how did the baby boom affect graduates of teacher training institutes as far as getting a job was concerned? Perhaps a comment made by one of my Peterborough Normal School masters summed it up rather succinctly. "Don't worry about your chances of getting a job," he told us. "If you can move a piece of chalk across a blackboard they'll hire you." He said this in 1949, just before the baby boomers started off to school. Obviously people in the know were aware that a market for many more teachers was just around the corner. To my knowledge none of us graduating that year had much trouble finding a school board to hire us. This was a far cry from times in the 1930s when some rural school three men boards received dozens of applications for teaching jobs.

Moreover, the days of the one-room rural school apprenticeship were drawing to a close. In fact, a few of my fellow graduates were hired on by large city boards of education.

The days of the one-room schools in our neck of the woods ended by 1970.

From what I read in the newspapers, in the matter of the teachers' job market the pendulum is now swinging in the other direction. With a substantial decrease in the number of elementary school children some schools have been closed and either sold or demolished. This in turn has resulted in teacher layoffs. Let us hope that this trend does not continue.

THE TWINS' TRICK

Some of you may recall when, as teachers or pupils you had twins in your classroom. If they were fraternal twins there was no difficulty in telling them apart, but if they were identical twins that was another matter. Sometimes a pair looked so much alike it seems that only their parents could tell which was Jimmy and which was Timmy. Talk about the proverbial two peas in a pod! When they were in a larger school with two classrooms at their age level the principal would usually assign one to each room which made it easier for all concerned to tell one twin from the other, at least when they were in their respective classrooms.

It happened one year that when a pair of indistinguishable identical twins arrived at a school I taught in, one of them, Joan, was placed in my grade 8 classroom and the other, Jean, was assigned to Bill Ward's room across the hall. They were a couple of bright young lassies who adapted well to their new school quite easily, soon became a most welcome addition to the school, and were liked by all. As well as being academically bright and socially quiet they had a rather wry sense of humour which later became all too apparent. When they were together on the playground dressed in the same garb it was virtually impossible for us at school to tell who was who.

The high point of the twins' year as far as the two grade 8 classes were concerned occurred one February afternoon. By that time of the school year routines were well established, nothing very exciting was going on in the school, and the February blahs were casting their sleepy spell on everyone. That's when the two girls put their trick into action, namely, they switched classrooms for the afternoon to see if they could take on each other's identity without anyone tripping them up in their act. I'm sure they rehearsed each other thoroughly in their respective seating locations, classroom routines, and the like. They even picked an afternoon when it would be a stay-at-your-desk situation, e.g., no Physical Education or library period.

The lessons proceeded quite normally and I think the two tricksters would have pulled it off successfully, but a simple class routine spoiled their plan. For several years I had arranged with my pupils to keep the notebooks in their desks in a certain order. (You may wish to refer back to chapter 7 at this point.) So when I asked the class to take out their History books, all of them, except Jean, simply counted down four books with their fingers without the need of bending over to check the name on the book, and zip, all the history books but one came out pronto.

Jean, however, took out a number of the books in the desk, sorted through them, found the right one, and then put the others back into the desk. She seemed quite flustered and became red in the face. I thought afterwards that she must have seen in her line of vision other pupils getting their books out so quickly and easily while she apparently was struggling to do so. By now she must have felt that she was becoming the centre of attention. At this point I did not suspect the twins of their ruse. My first thought was that Joan was having some sort of physical problem.

"Are you all right, Joan?" I asked.

"Yes," she replied rather sheepishly.

With that affirmative answer I started thinking there was

something strange going on here. Joan had followed that book removal routine for months without any problem, and suddenly this strange behaviour occurred. Then it hit me like a brick.

"Would you by any chance be Jean and not Joan?" I inquired.

Again she answered very meekly, "Yes."

Suddenly I let out a chuckle at the idea of two look-alike sisters playing a harmless game of deception and almost getting away with it. When the class saw me laughing they too figured out what was going on and we all had a good laugh over it.

When things had settled down a bit I said to Jean, "Get your coat and footwear and follow me." We crossed the hall to Bill Ward's room. After my rap on the door was answered by a pupil I walked in behind Jean and said, "Mr. Ward, here is your Jean. I would like my Joan back, please." There immediately followed another outburst of laughter with a resulting echo returning through the open door of my classroom.

To set the twins at ease I made a point of seeing them together before they left for home that day, and told them that we all enjoyed their playful prank. It certainly brightened up an otherwise dull day in the doldrums of winter.

WHO ARE YOU?

There are times in our lives when you meet a person, maybe passing by on the street or at some gathering together of people and immediately you get the feeling that you have met him/her somewhere before, but can't recall the circumstances. And the more you rack your brain to bring a name to mind, the more it eludes you. It's just as one songwriter wrote, "It seems we stood and talked like this before......but I can't remember where or when."

So you dig a little deeper into your memory but try as you may no light comes on. You attempt to put it aside but later during the day or maybe for a week or more this enigma keeps rising from your subconsciousness and you can't get rid of it. That's because it's a puzzle you would dearly love to solve. Maybe this is what Irving Berlin meant when he wrote that wonderful tune, You Keep Coming Back like a Song.

I suffered from this malaise when I moved to teaching at a different school. The very first time I saw the kindergarten teacher I just knew I had seen her somewhere before. She looked to be in her mid-forties and was actually one of the older members on a staff of fifteen, most of whom were much younger. In fact, four of them were fresh out of teachers' college. (The baby boom was burgeoning.) Being in a new school I was very busy getting used to new school routines, the layout of a different building, and the like, so it took a while to get to know the staff. Naturally I got to know those teaching near me first, and by meeting the others at recess or coming in off the parking lot I became acquainted with the entire staff. Since the kindergarten teacher, Mrs. Tanner, had her classroom in the basement and I was on the second floor, our paths hardly crossed at all. Yet of all the staff she was the one I wanted to find out more about. Just where had I seen her before? I pondered this riddle for some time and then the answer came to me at a school function beyond school property.

One of the lady teachers thought it would be a nice idea to have a social get-together at her house after school one day. It was an opportunity for staff members to get to know one another better in a non-school setting, and was held about the third week in September. This allowed us to enjoy a meal outdoors before fall weather brought on cooler and ever-darkening evenings. It was while we were standing around and chatting on a patio that I figured out my connection with Mrs. Tanner. Perhaps it was the way she walked, her voice tonality, or the way she moved her hands, but something suddenly rang a bell with me. I realized that this lady before me was my kindergarten teacher in my childhood days. I felt greatly elated, so much so that I blurted out without thinking, "Mrs. Tanner, now I remember you. You taught me in kindergarten back in 1934-35!"

Well! If looks could kill I would have died on the spot right then and there. I had offended her greatly in that I had indirectly given away how old she was. Surely all those people within hearing range were immediately making a few mental calculations and figuring out her age within a few years. For a few minutes I felt mortified by what I had done. Fortunately conversation soon picked up and the evening passed quickly and pleasantly.

The next year I was transferred to another school to fill a vacancy there. Up until her retirement I would see her at various meetings dealing with school matters, where we would renew fond memories of former days years ago. Yet every time I saw her I recalled that evening when I had "spilled the beans". A few years after she stopped teaching, the school I attended as a child held a centennial anniversary in 1989. As she was the only one of the teachers still alive from my school days there I asked her if she would honour us with her attendance and cut the cakes, beautifully iced in school colours, and serve them to former pupils and teachers who attended that event. She gladly accepted and enjoyed her day there very much. By 1976 that school had closed as an educational institution and changed over to a multi-purpose activity building. For several years Mrs. Tanner came back "home" to play bridge on a regular basis in the very room where she began her teaching career.

Interestingly enough, I had two kindergarten teachers in that afternoon class of 1934-35. The older one was a grandmotherly white-haired lady who retired two years later. Mrs. Tanner (then Miss Reynolds) on the other hand was a young, good-looking and vivacious lady whose personality won our hearts.

Why the two teachers? Apparently the school board at that time had a policy of bringing in a beginning kindergarten teacher as an apprentice to "learn the ropes" under the guidance of an experienced one – not a bad idea when you consider that kindergarten teaching requires a special knack. (Remember that book All I Needed to Know I Learned in Kindergarten?) In talking with a high school classmate years later who attended a different elementary school he said that Miss Reynolds was an assistant kindergarten teacher at his school in the mornings. So she was not only a well-liked teacher but a well-trained one also.

DID I PASS?

When I began teaching there were two federations that looked after the welfare of public school elementary teachers in Ontario; the Ontario Public School Men Teachers' Federation (OPSMTF) and the Federation of Women Teachers' Associations of Ontario (FWTAO). As early as the mid-1960s there were overtures to amalgamate them into one association, but it did not happen until the 1990s (finally!) Before then the men in our local branch of the federation held meetings about once a month consisting of the business at hand followed by light refreshments. The June meeting, however, was quite different. It was a sumptuous banquet, usually held in a rural setting, after which there was modest entertainment by some of the more talented members of our group.

One of these men was a principal nearing retirement, who had quite a collection of poetry books. Whenever the program committee asked him to give us a reading he was a very popular choice, as the poems he selected were most entertaining. Some were humourous, others were thought-provoking, but all that he read to us were quite poignant. We called him our poet laureate.

At one of our banquets he chose a poem with the most intriguing title – Did I Pass? Now with a title like that you might expect the individual in the poem doing the narrating was a pupil in the higher grades of elementary school, soliloquizing as to whether he would pass on to the next grade or repeat his year. Back when that poem was written this business of passing or repeating a grade was a matter of great concern for pupils because in those days promotion wasn't as "automatic" as it seems to be nowadays. When I think back to my days as a school pupil and in most years of my teaching it was not uncommon each year to note one or two pupils repeating a grade.

While we were talking among ourselves at the end of the

annual get-together we too thought that the message in the poem entitled Did I Pass? would be told by a senior pupil, but such was not the case. The poet cleverly withheld the age of the soliloquist at the start of his poem. At first it seemed that a youngster was talking, but as the poem unfolded he put in a few hints along the way, and we listeners soon realized that the speaker was not a pupil, but the classroom teacher!

Now you must admit that this poet handled the subject of passing from a unique point of view. Hearing that poem started me thinking just how would one go about judging whether or not a teacher "passed". That of course is one of the jobs of a school inspector (superintendent). As long as I still had my teaching contract at the end of the school year I could assume I passed. But throughout the rest of my teaching career that nagging question kept haunting me after the last school bell for the year rang – did I pass?

Here are some criteria by which a teacher's passing or failing might be based. I'm sure if a committee of teachers sat down to work on this topic they could add many more.

1. Did I instill in my pupils desirable attitudes and work habits, as well as teaching them knowledge and skills?

2. Did I have an air of friendship with the pupils but still remain in charge of the classroom?

3. Did I avoid appearing to be the fountain of all knowledge?

4. Did I give every subject in the curriculum its rightful amount of time and not spend extra time on my pet subject(s)?

5. Did I treat all those in my trust fairly, and not show favouritism?

6. Did I act as a person in authority in the classroom and not try

to be "one of the boys (girls)"?

7. Did I avoid treating my charges as a captive audience, and not tell them all about my past and present exploits?

8. Did I leave my home problems at home and as a result not give my pupils a bad day at school?

9. Did I not let myself get into a rut over the years, but instead try new approaches without "throwing out the baby with the bathwater"?

10. Did I come to school prepared for the day and not try to "wing it"?

11. Did I instill in my pupils that they were working for themselves, not for me?

Food for thought, fellow teachers, food for thought.

AN INTERESTING INTERVIEW

One evening in the spring of 1961 I saw in our local newspaper a picture of a man named John Thompson who had just celebrated his one hundredth birthday, and below it was an interesting account of his life. He had grown up in the Belleville area, enlisted with other volunteers to go west in 1885 to help put down the Riel Rebellion, and had actually seen Louis Riel not long after his capture. By coincidence I had just finished teaching this part of Canadian history and thought right away what a wonderful thing it would be if I could persuade him to come to our classroom for an interview with my grade 8 pupils. From the write-up in the paper I inferred that he was in very good shape for his age. It stated that he was still an ardent walker. In fact while in his eighties he walked one day to the village of Keene, about fourteen miles away to visit relatives and friends.

So the following Saturday morning I drove to his house situated beside River Road about a mile north of the city limits. It was one of a few small dwellings across the river from what is today the main campus of Trent University, which was founded in 1964. Other than these few houses the area was still very much a rural setting. I asked Mr. Thompson if he would agree to come to my classroom on an appointed afternoon to be interviewed by my pupils. He readily consented, we agreed on a time that I would arrive to drive him to the school, and as I left I repeated again slowly and clearly that I would be back to pick him up on the said day at 1:00 P.M. (Afternoon classes began in those days at 1:30.)

Back at school on Monday I informed the class about the upcoming interview and we immediately prepared for it. I explained that perhaps the best way to handle this might be to prepare questions, one per pupil, about Mr. Thompson's involvement in the rebellion. I would select what I considered to be the best questions, and with our guest seated at the front of the room I would call on each pupil in turn to ask his question.

Interview day arrived, and as I approached Mr. Thompson's house I was shocked to see a column of smoke rising, in my line of view, right over where his house was. Expecting the worst I stepped on the gas at once. I was relieved, however, to find that the building was not going up in flames, but I was confronted with another crisis – here was Mr. Thompson calmly throwing armloads of cedar brush on a blazing fire! Obviously he had either forgotten about his appointment or had mixed up his days.

What to do? I knew right then and there that we would not make it back to the school by 1:30. My first thought was to phone my principal, Mr. Green, and arrange with him to have my class supervised till I got back. Mr. Thompson declared that he had no phone, and since we could not just drive away from a fire in progress there was only one alternative left. I took off my tie, rolled up my sleeves and pitched in to feeding the fire with gusto, every so often looking anxiously at my watch. Between the two of us we soon had the fire to the point where we could douse it with water and leave safely.

As I drove speedily back into town I noticed that by now school had begun. I had not left the class any assigned work and wondered what they would be doing until I returned, especially since the principal's office and my room were separated only by one wall, and I knew that any loud sound was readily transferred from the one room to the other. I only hoped they weren't climbing the walls in there. As we approached the classroom door around 1:45 I was pleasantly surprised to find that all was quiet inside. Everyone had found something quiet to do while they were awaiting my return.

After introducing our guest and explaining briefly why we were late we began the interview, with Mr. Thompson and me seated at the front of the room. From time to time I repeated pupils' questions as he had difficulty with his hearing (his only apparent major physical problem). As he was a man of few words I interjected further questions to elicit more response from him on some interesting points. By and large he handled himself very well and he had quite a sense of humour. Also, he did not have to pause very long before returning answers; his memory was relatively sharp considering the fact that this rebellion had occurred seventy-five years before the interview. I taped the interview and still have a copy of it at home.

I had mentioned to Mr. Thompson at our first meeting that I could not drive him back home until school was over, but that he was welcome to sit at the back of the classroom and observe the class in action. While we finished the last lessons of the day I wondered what he thought of it all considering the fact that he had not attended school since the 1870s. No doubt it took him back to his early days and he likely made some interesting comparisons between then and now. After school I introduced him to Mr. Green, drove him home, and thanked him profusely for adding so much to our day.

The first thing next morning I apologized to the principal for being late the previous afternoon, explained the circumstances causing my tardiness, and said that I hoped the class hadn't been too noisy during my absence. His response was, "Oh! I didn't even know you were away. There was no undue noise coming from your room." Right after opening exercises I told the class what Mr. Green had said. I remarked to them that they could not have paid me a finer compliment. All in all it had been a great day.

AUDIO-VISUAL AIDS

When I began my teaching career in 1949 there were very few audio-visual aids to help in the teaching-learning situation. At the village school there was no library or reference books, nor were there any sound devices to assist in the learning process other than the live human voice. These factors made teaching conditions, shall we say, more primitive back then. By and large we had to make do with materials that were an on-going part of the classroom.

The most reliable standby we had was the blackboard, a device still found in almost every classroom to this day, and one that has been associated with schools since the 1800s. Just above the blackboards were three or four maps on rollers that could be pulled up or down like blinds. They served two purposes. Since easy to use duplicating machines were not available I sometimes arrived at school earlier in the morning than usual and wrote seatwork on some blackboards, pulled down the maps to cover it, and then let them up later when the class was ready to use the work behind them.

The other use maps served was of course in the teaching of history and geography. When I wanted to show the class the routes of various explorers I would make use of what were known in those days as chocolate bar maps. They were called this because a well known chocolate company of that era supplied them to schools on the condition that photos of their chocolate bar wrappers would be printed on the maps out on the oceans and well away from any islands therein. So while I was tracing the routes of Magellan and Drake in their circumnavigations of the world I wondered how many of them were paying attention to what I was doing and how many of them were gazing longingly at the jersey milk bar in the mid-Atlantic, the malted milk bar in the north Pacific, the jersey nut bar in the Indian Ocean, or the crispy crunch in the south Pacific. In my part of the world these maps were replaced in the 1960s by ones that were more up to date and had no advertising.

We had in our village school a rather cumbersome duplicating machine called a Gestetner. It was old and quite primitive. In fact, if I didn't know any better I'd say that it was one step up from Gutenberg's first printing press. On a stencil you could either type your information to be reproduced or write on it with a stylus, a metal pen with a very small rounded point that cut through the wax surface of the stencil. Then you affixed that stencil to the machine, squirted some black or blue ink on the right place on the roller, and turned the handle a few times to spread the ink evenly over the stencil. The machine was then put into gear and you cranked out your desired number of copies.

If you wanted to use that stencil again at a later date you had to blot off the ink when you removed it from the roller. This freed up the holes in the stencil made by the typewriter or stylus.

That old Gestetner had a personality all of its own – a mean one. If you looked at it the wrong way you ended up with ink on your hands. If you swore at it the ink would suddenly appear on your clothes. Early in my first year I watched some Home and School ladies preparing to run off copies of their monthly program letter on the Gestetner. (I wanted to pick up some hints on how to run it.) One was that the lady turning the handle wore an apron. Smart move!

These ladies were the only people I saw running the Gestetner. I gave up on my first try as it was too time consuming and messy. Instead I relied on the good old blackboard. In other schools later on I used better Gestetners to make arithmetic and grammar tests that could be used year after year.

Another duplicating device that was used at the time I started teaching was known as a hectograph. The interesting thing about this one was that you could make it right in your own home (or more likely, boarding house). You bought some gelatin and let it set in a small cookie tin with a lip around its perimeter. Then, with a special hectograph pencil containing a purple substance you drew you desired seatwork of phonics, arithmetic etc. on an ordinary piece of paper. This was pressed on to the sticky gelatin, which absorbed what was printed or drawn on the paper. From then on it was a matter of pressing down for a few seconds sheet after sheet of paper to transfer the seatwork from the gelatin to the paper. I'm told that if you did not remove the paper carefully the purple lines would smear quite easily. You could not expect to get many copies using this device but it worked quite well in one-room rural schools with anywhere from ten to thirty pupils from grades 1 to 8, where only three to six copies might be needed for any one grade level.

Both the Gestetner and the hectograph were rendered out of date by a newer device that was much faster and easier to operate. It was called a spirit duplicator because the liquid that was used to produce your desired copies was wood alcohol. There was a standing joke that if you used it for too long at a stretch you would walk away from that small duplicating room with a slight stagger. Nevertheless it did exude a rather intoxicating odour whenever it was overworked.

Operating it was a breeze. You typed, wrote, or drew the desired information on a master copy. This was automatically transferred to the back of the master by an underlying and attached sheet of carbon paper. You then removed this latter sheet, placed the master copy in a slot on the drum of the duplicator, locked it into place and cranked out the number of copies you wanted. Voila! Here at last was a duplicating machine that was ready to use almost instantly, there was no mess involved in running it, and in a couple of minutes you could run off enough copies for your whole class.

I was in a school in June 2008 to look at the latest type of duplicating machine in use in the local school system. This up-to-date device, a photocopier, is almost robotic in nature. It can three-hole punch paper, staple sheets together, print on both sides of the paper, and use up to four different colours all at the same time. Also there is no cranking by hand or counting the number of copies you need. Just press the desired number on a key pad and the machine counts them out and then stops on its own. We truly live in an age of technological wonders.

A different type of visual aid known as the overhead projector came into use in our part of the world in the mid-1950s. You drew or typed information on a clear sheet of plastic called a transparency, laid it on the projector, turned on a light, and it shone that information on to a screen mounted in the classroom. The beauty of this device was that you could lay one transparency on top of another to show the development of something. This was very useful in some aspects of mapwork and science lessons. I often used it to show pupils how to edit compositions.

Again in June 2008 I witnessed the latest development in overhead projectors, called a smartboard. This has the same function as the overhead projector but it runs from a computer, which means that the information it projects can more easily be stored for future use.

The Home and School Association in my first school provided the staff with a reel to reel tape projector which we used for recording sound. This was great when you wanted to let a choir or instrumental group know what they sounded like, and from that make adjustments to improve on the outcome of their music. When I had individual children speak into this device each one was simply amazed at hearing what they sounded like "outside of their heads". This rather cumbersome machine was made obsolete by cassette tapes, those wonderful, small packages about 4" by 2½" by ¼".One of them plays for about ninety minutes and can be operated by a small machine that can clip on to your belt while you walk, skate, play golf, etc. Do we really appreciate the technological marvels of our modern world? We've come a long way, audio-visually, in the last sixty years.

PHYSICAL? EDUCATION?

A game known as slo-pitch, a variety of softball, has become very popular during the last half century and today there are many men and women playing it in leagues in different parts of our country. I was first introduced to it in the mid-1940s when our Physical Education teacher taught it to us at the local high school. It became quite the in thing in elementary schools in this area by the 1960s and I still see it being played nowadays at an elementary school close to my home.

Now slo-pitch is an interesting game to watch or play. It differs from ordinary softball in that the pitcher lobs the ball slowly over the home plate as the name of the game suggests, so that the batter has a far better chance of hitting it than he would in a regular softball game. As a result this produces more work for the team behind the pitcher. Slo-pitch might seem like a good activity for children but as I see it the game is not suited for Physical Education classes in school hours.

I make this statement for different reasons. If the teacher in charge is not an authoritative person here's what happens. In a typical class of thirty pupils the six infield positions are automatically claimed by the most athletic boys while the other boys and the girls on that team, all nine of them, are relegated to the outfield. So the six players who least need the exercise hog the infield, the area closest to the action, while all the rest are banished to the more remote section known as the outfield. While two or three outfielders might be keenly waiting to field the balls that are hit beyond the infield, what do the rest of them do? Being totally disinterested in the game at hand they look around for other diversions to fill in the time such as conversing with one another, looking upward at interesting cloud formations scudding across the sky, or examining the flora and fauna beneath their feet. Having little to do out there makes them totally bored.

Secondly, in all the years I've seen slo-pitch played at the elementary school level I don't recall observing pupils being taught the skills needed to improve their playing and enjoyment of the game. This includes how to hold the bat and swing it properly, how to throw and catch a ball, and how to position your body in front of a grounder so that it does not get past you. Natural athletes learn these things instinctively; the rest of us have to be taught them.

In addition, unless the teacher in charge acts as the umpire of the game the pupils are simply learning mob rule. A case in point is, when a thrown ball and a runner arrive at a given base at about the same time, is the runner safe or out? If the teacher doesn't make the call, then the pupils do. Then it becomes a noisy contest with the batting side shouting safe while the fielding side yells out. Then a constant din of "SAFE! OUT!

SAFE! OUT!" follows. Perhaps the only exercise some pupils get during the game is a good workout for the lungs.

So the trouble with slo-pitch at the elementary school level is that it does not meet the criteria of Physical Education. That is in most cases it is neither physical nor is it education. The "exercise" most children get during the game is walking leisurely out to the field and back beside the home plate as the innings change. And without any instruction from the teacher the pupils are not learning much. The game can be a real copout for the teacher – just take the class and equipment out to the playground, stand back and watch, and let the kids go to it.

By no means am I the first person to realize that slo-pitch is not a suitable activity for Physical Education classes in school. Almost fifty years ago a trustee on the local public school board of education was driving by a school and noticed a number of children standing on the playground and seemingly doing nothing. (It obviously wasn't recess time.) Being curious she phoned the principal about it. She got her answer and he got his earful. The next day he sent a note around to the staff stating the gist of his conversation with the trustee, that from now on slo-pitch was not to be played in Phys. Ed. Classes, and that henceforth these class periods should involve more pupil movement. Amen!

A LETTER TO MY FORMER PUPILS

287 Greenlawn Ave.

Peterborough, Ont.

K9H 5K7

Dear former pupils,

May I take this opportunity to say hello to all of you, those whom I have met since my retirement in 1984 and the many I haven't seen since you left elementary school. As you are well aware there has been a lot of water over the dam since then.

It has been nice meeting some of you at various school reunions in recent years, and if you should happen to become a member of the planning committee for one of these happy occasions, please invite me to come. I love reunions, where we can talk over old times together. I have also enjoyed chancing upon some of you in your places of work, on city streets, and at various functions around town.

One of your number came up to me in a restaurant recently and introduced herself. When she told me the school and grade wherein I taught her we figured out that we hadn't seen each other in fifty-five years! I was flattered to think that she recognized me after all that time. If we should meet and you tell me who you are I may not recognize you. After all, you will have changed greatly over anywhere from twenty-five to almost sixty years. Remember also that there are a lot of you to recall by name. I figured out once that I taught over a thousand pupils during my career.

I hope I taught you more than just knowledge, and that you remember some of the other things I tried to impart to you. Do you recall some of those placards that were posted at the front of the classroom? e.g., For whom are you working? Did you earn your KASH to day? and Our class motto is I can and I will.

Perhaps this is a good time to explain, especially to those pupils I had towards the latter part of my career, why I instituted certain classroom routines which I know puzzled some pupils. First was asking you to stand to answer a question. There were three good reasons for this. In the first place other pupils could hear you better, especially if you spoke softly. Secondly, I was preparing you for speaking at public functions in your later years. Many adults do not like having to stand up among a group of people to express their views. So hopefully, standing up to speak among your classmates would help you overcome this phobia. Talking while on your feet may have put you in the spotlight of course, but this was intentional for your own betterment. Finally, there was a physical reason why I had you stand to answer. If pupils sit at a desk for very long they get fidgety. I found that having pupils stand to answer questions was a quick and easy way for them to wear off that restlessness with a bit of unrealized physical activity.

Another routine which I found out indirectly that some pupils thought was antiquated was having pupils say yes sir or no sir to a male teacher, rather than just a plain yes or no. If I had been a female teacher I would have expected the reply yes Mrs. Paterson. To me that was simply a time-honoured way of showing respect. Nowadays I don't hear the words please, thank you, excuse me, and I'm sorry as much as I used to. I make no apologies for having tried to teach good manners to my pupils.

If you and I were back together in the classroom today we both would find many changes in the curriculum. A ready example is the form of this letter you are now reading. It is different from the one that I taught you where the address, closing, and signature were placed beside the right hand margin. Today all parts of a letter begin at the left side of the paper making it neat, simple, and practical.

In the same way all of us have changed just as the leaves on a tree do through the seasons of the year. While we may not be as active physically as we once were perhaps it is safe to say that we have mellowed just as a ripened fruit does. It is my wish for you that you may flourish in your remaining years.

You came to my classroom in September in various sizes, shapes, desires, and outlooks. Each of you was very important to me, because when you think about it, you were my bread and butter. If fate had not brought us together my life would certainly have been different. Without your presence I don't know literally what I would have done.

In conclusion remember this, that no matter what may become of us you will always be a part of me, and I shall always be a part of you.

Best wishes to all,

Murray Paterson

RAINY RECESSES

You will remember numerous times in your elementary school days when you   were not let outside for recess because it was raining. Instead you stayed in the classroom and had what was known as a rainy recess. In many schools the principal announced this decision by giving the recess bell a second, short push. You probably didn't like rainy recesses because you were still confined to the four walls of your room and wanted a change of scenery. Your teachers felt the same way too as many of them looked forward to socializing in the staff room and enjoying a cup of coffee.

At the start of a rainy recess most pupils got a drink of water, headed for the washroom, and then spent the rest of the time gathering into small groups and talking. Teacher supervision varied. Some teachers remained the full recess in their classrooms, thereby ensuring a reasonable degree of law and order. Others went to the staff room long enough to get a cup of coffee and immediately returned with it back to the classroom. Still others went to stay in the staff room, leaving the class on their own, and hoping the room would still be in one piece when they returned at bell time.

Personally, I had no problem with staying in the classroom throughout a rainy recess. For the first third of my teaching career either there were no staff rooms in some schools or if there were teachers didn't congregate in them on a regular basis. Staying in one's classroom was the thing to do in my teaching experience back in the 1950s and early sixties when it rained at recess.

I found it interesting to watch what different pupils did with their time during a rainy recess. The odd solitary book lover would reach into the desk, pull out a library book, and enjoy another chapter before the bell rang again. There would usually be a small group of athletic boys standing at the windows and gazing out, longing to be outside playing at softball, basketball, or some other active endeavour. Most pupils, however, would be clustered in small groups chatting about anything and everything. By observing the facial expression, language, and body stance of the pupils in a non-teaching situation rainy recesses gave a teacher the chance to gain some insight as to what made various pupils tick.

One recess when the class was kept indoors due to the rain I came up with an idea. It became known in our classroom as rainy recess arithmetic and it goes like this. You take a pack of cards and remove the aces, tens, and face cards. One pupil, the dealer, sits behind a desk while four or five others are seated in a semicircle facing him. The dealer then lays out five cards face up, side by side. The pupils mentally add up these numbers and the first person who says the right answer gets a point. The dealer records the accumulated number of points per pupil, and the first person to amass five points becomes the new dealer. It's as simple as that. There are certain variations to this game.

Subtraction---$53 - 7 = $ "46"

Multiplication--- $74 \times 8 = $ "592"

Division ---54 divided by $7 = $ "7 and 5" (remainder)

It was usually the dealer's choice as to which variation his group played. At no time did I coerce any pupil to play this rainy recess game. I simply introduced it to them and it took off on its own from there.

Now, how did the pupils like this new game? Just before recess one enthusiastic class I had would look out the window on those on and off showery days, waiting eagerly to see whether or not there would be a rainy recess. When that second, short bell announced "Stay inside" a quick, subdued cheer went up right away and before I had a chance to say anything they started setting up the room in order to play rainy recess arithmetic.

Surely this was a unique recess experience. Not only were they finding enjoyment in playing a game they liked but they kept themselves occupied at a worthwhile activity. To top it all off they were improving their skills in the fundamentals of arithmetic at, of all times, recess!

Looking back on it I wished I'd taken out a patent on this idea. I might have made a fortune.

REPORT CARDS

Whenever report cards are issued at various times during the school year they are met with some anxiety on the part of parents and pupils. The former want to know what sort of headway their child is making while the latter wonder what reaction this report will produce from their parents. As a report card is the most formal notice a mother and father receive about their child's progress it is a matter of concern when Johnny or Mary hands that informative document over to their parents.

Before these reports go home is a very busy time for teachers, who have had much work to do in testing pupils, marking papers, and tabulating results. Then there is the matter of entering comments wherein the teacher gives reasons for a pupil's success or lack thereof, makes suggestions for improvement, and writes a synopsis of the pupil's deportment in school.

In past years I've witnessed both letter ratings (ABCDs) and percentages to indicate on report cards what sort of progress pupils were making in the various subjects. There's no doubt that it's easier for a teacher to give a pupil, let us say in science, an A for excellent (75-100), B for good (67-74), C for fair (60-66), or D for poor (below 60) than to arrive at a numerical rating of say

82%, 68%, or 53%. In the lower elementary school grades I can see the advantage of letter ratings but by grades 6, 7, and 8 I feel that percentage ratings give a more accurate picture of how a pupil is doing in his/her school work.

Actually, when a teacher with a few years experience gets a new pupil part way through the year it doesn't take more than a couple of weeks to figure out what sort of letter ratings he's worth on his next report card. By his attentiveness, participation, work habits, and his interaction with his new classmates, the teacher knows whether he's an A, B, C, or D pupil.

By using numerical ratings both the pupil and parents can see gains or losses not apparent when letter ratings are used. For example, let's say a pupil gets three As in a certain subject in three reports one year. How's he doing? If numbers had been used – 75, 94, 80, that would present a more accurate picture. Or suppose another child receives three Cs in a subject over the year. Is he progressing at all? If you translate those three Cs to 61, 64, and 66 his progress is immediately apparent. I've heard some teachers say that you can't fine tune percentages on report cards, that you have to stick with the broad bands of A, B, C, or D. I don't agree with that. First of all let us assume that we are talking about an ordinary, average class, not gifted pupils or slow learners. If a teacher establishes a "you're here to learn" attitude, motivates pupils well, prepares his lessons diligently, and sets a variety of tests that are fair (not too easy or grueling) then I think he can arrive at a percentage rating that is right on the money.

Looking at an old grade 8 report card that I have from the 1950s I note that the standings in art, music, and physical education are entered as letters, not numbers. I could certainly go along with that as these subjects are difficult to appraise numerically at the elementary school level. If I were a pupil in school again I would hope that my art rating would not be based on what sort of masterpiece I could produce but on my ability to utilize the information the teacher gave me to improve upon my drawings, paintings, etc. Likewise in music I trust that my rating would not be a matter of how well I sang or played an instrument but of how well I was trying to learn and apply music theory, which is what makes music a language all of its own. Finally I would like to think that my physical education letter would not be a question of how athletic I was as much as what effort I put forth into trying to improve my skills in physical exercises and games.

At one time the school board I worked for had another interesting figure on its report cards. Directly below the pupil's average percentage for the term was the class average. This gave parents some additional information. If the class average was 83% then that set of high marks their child brought home didn't mean too much. On the other hand if the class average was 62% this could mean that the teacher wasn't doing a very good job of teaching, or that his tests were not geared to the pupils' capabilities, or that he was an extremely hard marker. A child bringing home a report card with a 72% average in this case would obviously be doing quite well.

Looking back over my career I find it very strange that in all those thirty-five years I never once saw in print or heard any educators discuss what the average percentage for the report cards of a group of normal children should be. Upon looking over some old sets of marks I still have in my filing cabinet I find that the average   percentage appears to be about 67%.

Some teachers will remember a set of OSR cards (Ontario School Records, till circa 1970), folders for all children in a class containing pertinent information about those pupils. Near the end of June teachers were required to fill in the final percentage each pupil received in the list of subjects on every card. For three years at one school I found it interesting to compare the marks I wrote down for my grade 8 classes with those of a well-respected grade 7 teacher whose pupils I inherited. It pleased me to no end to find that my marks very rarely were five points above or below her entries.

The subjects listed on report cards when I taught did not change much over the years. There were times, however, when a new one was added for some reason or other. In the late 1950s one entitled Literary Appreciation suddenly appeared. I don't recall ever seeing in writing or hearing at meetings just what it was. Looking up these two words in a dictionary I figured out that it meant the evaluation of superior books and writings. Right away the question in my mind was how do you measure to what degree a person appreciates certain things. Who is to say that one person values sight, hearing, mobility, etc. more than another? I think that people don't appreciate many of the common things in their lives until they lose them. In the early 1980s we had another new subject to be evaluated, namely Listening Skills. I suppose teachers have a fairly good idea as to how well each of their pupils listens, but getting down to the nitty-gritties, just how do you measure listening? I asked a superintendent about this at a meeting once, and he merely sloughed it off. Fortunately neither of these two "subjects" lasted very long on report cards.

The last section of the report to be completed was the area in which teachers commented on a pupil's progress. This consisted mainly of reasons why a pupil was doing well or poorly in the various subjects, and steps that should be taken to bring about improvement in areas of weaknesses. Sometimes comments about a child's deportment were included also. In my time these comments were handwritten, unlike those that are typed nowadays. I feel that the remarks we made in handwriting had a more personal touch than the present-day typewritten ones.

I wrote up my comments in this manner. First I jotted down in rough any ideas that came into my mind about a certain pupil's marks. Then after numbering them in a logical order I composed my comments on a sheet of paper. This was done for about six reports. By then my brain became slightly addled with too many thoughts going around in my head at the same time. So

I'd take a short, physical break, come back and revise these comments, and then copy them on to the report cards. If I tried to write up too many reports at one time I found myself wanting to repeat earlier comments that were not applicable to other pupils.

Let me conclude with an interesting anecdote. I usually told my classes that I'd like their report cards brought back to the school in about a week. This gave some of them time to show their various relatives how they were doing in school. At the end of one term Andy took home a less than flattering report card. Within a few days all the other reports had been returned to me but his. Upon asking him repeatedly for it I received from him not reasons for his tardiness but alibis. (At this point some teachers will recall those "the dog ate my homework" fibs.) Sensing something fishy I phoned Andy's home and informed his father, whom I knew to be a rather blustery and domineering man, about the situation. Did he ever get riled up! He told me in language very loud and abusive that he had not yet seen Andy's report card. Andy's game obviously was to delay as long as possible that fateful moment when he would have to show the report card to his father.

Next day Andy handed me his report card duly signed by his father. I did not say anything to him. That was not necessary, as I knew his father would have told him all that needed to be said.

THE PRINCIPAL SUMMONS

It's strange what lengths some people in authority will go in order to gain popularity. Take the case of the jovial principal I worked under in one school.

I taught in one of the last schools in the city that did not yet have a public address system. This created a problem if a message from the office were such that it should be relayed to all staff members right away. That was not much of an issue in the elementary school I attended or the first school where I taught as both had only ten classrooms, and it didn't take long for the principal to deliver his message in person. Also, things were less hectic back then and there was not the need for a lot of information coming from the principal.

Now the summoning principal, Mr. White, had a clever way to get news to his staff quickly. He used pupil messengers. In September he assigned some of his grade 8 pupils, one per classroom, to deliver his information to their respective classrooms. This could be accomplished in a few minutes and saved the principal much time and effort in getting messages to fourteen teachers spread out over two storeys and a basement (the latter was in use as the baby boom was at its zenith in the late 1950s).

So one quiet afternoon in February about half way between school assembly and recess my runner appeared at the classroom door. "Mr. White would like to see you in his office as soon as possible." Well! This was shocking to say the least, and I suspected some dire news was in store. I only hoped it did not concern my family in any way. I stopped the work in progress, quickly assigned the class some seatwork, and strode through the door.

On my way to the office I noticed two other staff members heading in that same direction. Aha, I thought, there must be something going on that concerns the whole school, and I began to think what it could be. Now this was well before the time of bomb threats and guns in schools, and my first thought was that the school was caught up in some sort of epidemic that required immediate action.

Arriving at the office we found that a few of the staff were already there, some seated and others standing, facing Mr. White, who was seated behind his desk. Now Mr. White had an unusual habit whenever he was anxious or upset. He would take the heel of his hand and rub it upwards on his forehead and then over the front of his close-cropped gray hair. As each new teacher entered the room he gave his forehead another rub. This was a habit he was well aware of, as I found out that afternoon. We could also observe him counting as one teacher after another came into the office. He seemed to be impatient to get us all together.

When we were all assembled before him he uttered in a low voice, "You must wonder why I called all of you down here at this time." With that he leaned back in his chair, looked around at us, and gave his forehead two more quick rubs. We awaited the worst news. He suddenly said, "You all look worried." Then he reached into his top desk drawer, pulled out a box, opened it up and declared, "Here, relax and have a chocolate." What a prank! After we were finished eating our chocolate (I said eating, not enjoying) he said, "There, that's done. Now you can get back to work." Which we did.

We were not amused. In talking over this incident with other teachers at recess the kindest thing we had to say was that Mr. White had his heart in the right place and that he was a good actor. His timing, however, was dreadful. Had he given any thought as to what he might have been interrupting by his choice of timing for this antic? Here are some of the activities he might have cut off suddenly by his summons: a grade 8 volleyball game in which the score was tied fourteen all, and the teams were just ready to play for the game-winning point, a grade 7 class to which the teacher, reading an epic poem, was at the critical moment when the hero and the villain were fighting it out near the edge of a cliff, a grade 5 class half way through watching a time-lapse photography film on the growth of a plant, and a grade 3 class, containing four impish boys, part way through a spatter-painting lesson.

We all agreed that he should have asked us to come to his office at the start of recess. At that time of the afternoon we would have enjoyed his caprice. What can be a pleasant occasion at one time can be a disaster at another. Timing is so important.

BOOKS AND BOOK REPORTS

How would we ever get along in our modern society without books? They inform, inspire, comfort, and amuse us. Despite the prevalence of television and computers today books have several advantages. A book is lightweight and thus is easy to carry from place to place, it doesn't take up much space in a knapsack, room, or automobile, it needs virtually no preparation to use, and it can be used to fill in those periods of waiting before some appointments. A wise man once said that a dull person is one who can't (or doesn't want to) read on a rainy day. Think of all the knowledge and pleasure a person amasses over a lifetime through the reading of books.

As a teacher one of my fondest memories concerning books began right in my first year of teaching. While the class was busy at some assignment at their desks I would call a pupil to come to a quiet corner at the back of the room. The two of us would sit at a table where he handed me a book he had finished reading and then proceeded to tell me in a few minutes what it was all about. After that I opened up the book in various places and asked two or three questions. e. g., What part did Mr. Graham play in this book? Who won the automobile race in chapter 5? What kind of fish did Bill catch? I usually ended up by asking the pupil how he liked the book. When we were finished there was no doubt in my mind as to how well that pupil had read the book concerned. Another reason why I liked this "interview" approach was that it gave both the pupil and me a chance to interact with each other one on one. This was not easy to do in a large class with two grades in it. In my first year I had forty-seven pupils in that class.

My readers had access to books from two sources. First was the children's section of the village library. We also had a children's books company that periodically sent out advertisements of their latest books with their prices and an order form. I collected the money from my pupils, mailed the order form, and in a short time the books arrived at the school.

When I moved to teaching in the city I was soon informed that pupils were to write so many book reports each year. The purpose behind this I suppose was to provide proof that pupils had actually read the books they had selected. Since the era of schools with their own libraries had not yet arrived books were brought to the school on a regular basis by librarians from the public libraries in town. From then on each class in the school had a scheduled library period.

So now, along with all the other reading a teacher does in his/her school-related work I felt that reading all these book reports might just be the straw that broke the camel's back. As I recall it these reports were not given any rating or evaluation, but I was to read them just to ascertain that some books had been read by my pupils. Then one day something from the subconscious part of my mind came to light. I remembered those short oral book reports from my first years of teaching and decided to implement them again, only this time with a new twist. Instead of having each pupil telling me privately about a book I decided to have him/her talk to the whole class about it.

I felt that this approach had several advantages. First of all every pupil in the class was "on stage" for a few minutes while telling us about a book. This is something that does not happen very often in school, especially with introverted children. Hopefully it would help bring them out of their shells. Also, a more prominent place for reading was developed in pupils' minds when they listened to a speaker sharing his/her knowledge of a book. I noticed that some pupils did such a good job of "selling" their books that at the next library period those books were immediately sought out. From my point of view this new scheme freed up more time for me. Bear in mind that in those days we had no preparation time during school hours as teachers do nowadays.

Finally, it was an excellent prelude for public speaking, which was a prominent part of the English program in the Peterborough schools. It helped to develop confidence and poise in the speakers. I did not permit pupils to have notes in their hands while they reported on the books they had read. Actually this was not necessary because, assuming that they had read their books they could easily remember to tell their classroom audience what the setting of a book was, give a description of its main characters, and then sum up the plot briefly. Using this method of reporting about a book it would have been very difficult for a pupil to bluff his/her way through it while facing both classmates and teacher, without having read the book first. I stressed with them not to give away the whole story, but to leave their audience in suspense so that some of them would want to get their hands on those books to find the outcome of its plot. It is my opinion that this method of reporting on library books was very satisfactory to both the pupils and their teacher.

HAVE YOU EARNED YOUR KASH TODAY?

Remember when you came home from school, sat down at your evening meal, and one of your parents asked, "What did you learn at school today?" Your immediate answer was probably, "Nothing."

It's a very fair question for parents to ask their offspring how they are progressing at school, and the reason children often give such a quick, negative answer is that they probably don't really know what they have learned, especially in their elementary school years. For example let's say that a grade 8 class has just finished studying Wordsworth's poem, The Daffodils. You can't expect these pupils to tell their parents that evening at the supper table, "Today I learned that I can use my memory to bring back pleasant images from my past experiences."

So this raises the question what do children actually learn in school. Perhaps this can be summed up by a mnemonic. (Aren't mnemonics marvelous? How could we older folks cope without them?) This simple memory device is the home made word KASH – K for knowledge, A for attitude, S for skills, and H for habits.

Knowledge is the easiest one to explain, and provides ready answers to that perennial question at the first of this chapter. Some examples are: the names of the provinces and capital cities of Canada, the meaning of area and volume, the important battles of the War of 1812, the names of the parts of a flower, Sir Francis Drake's route on his voyage around the world, and how the Great Lakes affect the climate of Southern Ontario. If a poll were taken as to what children learn in school I think most people, on looking back at their school days, would put knowledge at the top of the list. At the elementary school level this factual information is found mainly in three subjects:

History, Geography, and Science. In my teaching days we called them the content subjects.

You will not likely find the word attitude on a school report card, but this intangible attribute affects not only school children but all of humanity from age one to one hundred and one. One dictionary defines attitude as a person's disposition to other people and things. It's how you regard what you experience in the world around you, or your outlook on people, places, and events. Perhaps it can be best understood by pairing up some of its opposite characteristics: happy/grumpy, gentle/overbearing, sharing/self-centred, curious/indifferent, I think I can/I give up, give it your best shot/what's the use.

Now I think we would all agree that a positive or negative attitude is primarily instilled by parents in the home but a teacher has considerable influence in molding a child's attitude. Here are some ways a teacher can improve children's attitudes: teaching teamwork – passing the ball down the field or gym rather than moving it all by yourself, teaching the pupils to use the words please, thank you, and I'm sorry (very much reinforced when the teacher himself uses these terms in class management), teaching how to accept both victory and defeat in contests gracefully, and studying desirable role models in history and literature. I'm sure we can all think of teachers who were either a positive or negative influence in shaping our attitudes.

Skill is defined as the ability to do something well. In teaching, this is the "how to" area of the curriculum and examples of skills taught in school abound. How to: hold a pencil, read and write, draw a tree, recognize a sentence, play a musical instrument, deliver a speech, find a percentage of a number, and compose a unified paragraph. Arithmetic is mainly a skill subject as it is a matter of manipulating numbers so as to arrive at a desired conclusion.

At what point can you say that you have mastered a new skill? It likely occurs when you can execute that skill with only a minimum of mental effort. Remember the joy you felt when you could first tie a bow in your shoelaces all by yourself, or read a clock? When a youngster learns a new skill at school it pleases not only him but his teacher as well.

A habit is defined as a customary practice that a person exhibits. Habits can be either good or bad, and in a school setting I'm referring to work habits, not personal ones. Here is proof that some good work habits have been instilled by the teacher. The pupils keep orderly desks, learn to listen attentively to the lesson at hand, tackle the work they are doing with gusto, check over finished work for errors (arithmetic and composition!), and use spare time wisely when they finish an assignment early (a library book in every desk is great). For good work habits to happen the teacher must set the example. It's a case of do as I do and not do as I say. Whether they like it or not teachers are role models for their classes at all times, and pupils will pick up not only their mental habits but physical ones as well e.g., posture, speech, voice intonation, and deportment.

I witnessed a very good example of this while on yard duty one day. Two young girls were talking to each other very rapidly. I said to them, "I'll bet you two are in Miss Johnston's room."

"Yes," they answered. "How did you know?"

"Oh, I figured it out," I replied. (At all times Miss Johnston spoke a mile a minute.) Unlike a good hockey referee a teacher is in the limelight at all times in the classroom. Like attitudes, work habits are hard to measure but they can have a lasting effect after school days are over.

I used to post a sign over the blackboard at the front of the classroom – HAVE YOU EARNED YOUR KASH TODAY? From time to time I would point to it just before dismissal time and say, "If you earn your KASH now you will get more CASH later on in life."

SNOW DAYS

Every profession, trade, or job has its own language, and teachers certainly have theirs. In their everyday conversation they use certain words and phrases that may not be familiar to lay people, such as preparation time, curriculum, yard duty, indoor recess, and content subjects. Some time after my retirement a new one was added, namely snow days. Now a snow day is one in which it is deemed unsafe for a school bus driver to go along his route to pick up school pupils for two reasons. Either there has been a freezing rain or a heavy snowfall overnight, and the municipalities concerned have not yet been able to make the roads safe for driving. Whenever in an evening the weather forecasters anticipate foul weather conditions some children are glued to the radio early next morning with baited breath to find out if their school bus has been cancelled or not. After all, there's nothing like getting an unexpected holiday.

Now just who determines whether or not there will be a snow day? Apparently it is a joint decision among the board of education staff, the bus company, and the bus drivers. Interestingly enough, one area may have a snow day while one a few miles away may not. Compare a bus that goes over fairly flat terrain near a city and along a major road that is kept plowed and/or sanded during the night, with another bus that goes through hilly country on remote township roads that are not serviced till later in the day.

People from my generation never experienced a snow day. That's not because we didn't have icy or snow-covered streets and roads. I'm sure many of you can well remember sliding your way to school with great relish on ice-covered thoroughfares. As far as snow depth goes all elementary school children lived within walking distance of a school, either to a graded school in an urban setting or to a one-room rural school in the countryside. We never gave any thought to walking through deep snow. We simply put on our boots or overshoes and away we went.

Kids love trudging through snow. Every winter I watch them coming along our street shortly before bell time. They're not walking on the plowed road but alongside it across our front lawns, climbing up and down the mountains of snow we've shovelled up beside our driveways.

Mind you, we have had some dandy snowfalls to contend with in the Peterborough area over the last sixty-odd years. One February morning in 1945 we woke to find our street completely covered in a pure white, deep blanket of snow such that it was impossible to discern where the sidewalk and the road met. Cars were few and far between in that wartime era and streets were not always cleared of snow back then in time for people to get to work. I got to high school the easiest way possible by skiing seven blocks down the middle of Peterborough's main street on an unsullied mantle of white. It was a lovely experience.

In 1947 we had another snowstorm. Afterwards I was on my way north from Peterborough to Lakefield to play hockey after school. (We never played school sports in school hours back then!) A short way along the trip we witnessed something incredible. Just north of where you turn right to approach the entrance to Trent University there had been some very heavy drifting of snow down a short stretch of the highway. The county road crew had carved out a channel through this deep impediment but it was wide enough for only one vehicle to drive through at a time. As we crawled slowly through what appeared to be a tunnel we were utterly amazed to note that, even though we were sitting well above ground level on bus seats, we could not see over the top of the snow channel on either side of the bus.

Then on the morning of April 3, 1975 we were surprised by a late-season heavy dump of snow. I think the city road maintenance men were surprised also, as the streets were not cleared of snow till much later in the day. (Had the plows been put out to summer pasture too soon?) I still have a photograph my wife took of me skiing to school that morning down the middle of our street.

The mother of all snowfalls in a twenty-four hour period came on December 11-12, 1992. Southern Ontario was hit with a massive overnight snowfall and the Peterborough area had the distinction of receiving more snow at that time than any other part of Ontario. When it had stopped snowing by dawn on December 12 we had received two feet of fresh snow. I was plowing snow back then for one of my sons who had a snowplowing business, and let me tell you, I was a pretty popular fellow as I drove around town that day. Whereas I used to count snowplow trucks for a diversion as I made my rounds, by late afternoon that day I noticed three plow trucks being led away by tow-trucks. They had literally been worked to death because of all that deep snow. The same thing happened occasionally to horses that drew snowplows along sidewalks in Peterborough prior to 1965. After a very heavy snowfall the odd horse would drop in its traces from overwork.

But the snowy day I remember best in connection with schools occurred on February 25, 1960. Once again the city woke that morning after another heavy invasion of the white stuff during the night. It was too deep for my old flivver to handle, and the radio reported that the city buses were not running, so that left me with just one other alternative – hoof it. I left quite early and arrived at school after an exhilarating walk through a winter wonderland one and a half miles (2.5 km) in length. It reminded me a bit of the comment a rural resident is said to have made about his school days. "I had to walk two miles to school every day and it was uphill both ways."

The number of pupils in all classes was greatly depleted, so the principal came up with an ingenious idea. We were going to have a contest making snow castles. First he divided the pupils into a few equal groups, not by grade, as a senior class would then have won hands down. Each group contained roughly the same number of pupils from each of grades 1 to 8. He then allotted each group its fair share of playground, not that there was any scarcity of raw material available. Meanwhile the caretakers had rounded up all the shovels, pails, and anything else by which snow could be moved about.

Then the children went right to it while we teachers looked on from the sidelines. It was quite a spectacle to watch. The groups did not rush in their endeavours. After all there was no prize awarded for the largest or highest mound of snow constructed. What we were pleased to observe as teachers was the way the older pupils in each group helped the younger ones. They were more concerned about working together as a team than building the biggest castle. It was very reminiscent of pupils in one-room schools of earlier days where all the pupils co-operated in completing a project, e.g., the annual Christmas concert or arbour day activities. The children worked at two subjects that morning, one was obviously Physical Education and the other was what used to be known as Social Studies, the interaction of people, one with another. The staff really enjoyed watching these team efforts.

By noon hour the city streets were navigable again, and the school had close to a full complement that afternoon. No doubt those who built the snow castles told the late arrivals about how much fun they had missed that winter morning.

A WELCOME VISITOR

We had a most unusual visitor to our city school for part of one year. It all began while my grade 8 class was busy doing some seatwork and I was marking the register one autumn afternoon. All of a sudden I heard what seemed like two or three chirps from a bird, but it was not coming from outside the school. My first thought was that someone in the classroom across the hall had brought a canary into the building for a science lesson that afternoon.

Then it gave a slightly longer call, and I realized that it was not a bird that was singing. It was a cricket! Those high-pitched chirps which sound somewhat like a bird with a raspy throat were all too familiar to me. Over the years my family enjoyed their trilling sound on warm summer evenings at the cottage.

This time I looked at the class to see if there was any reaction to our singing visitor. A few of them looked back curiously, wondering no doubt about what to them was a strange sound, not one associated with an urban setting. So we stopped what we were doing and talked crickets for a while. I told them that our guest was a male, as only male crickets produce this unique sound. They were amused when I informed them that by means of his tune he was looking for a bride. Unlike birds, however, the sound is not produced by the voice but by rubbing one forewing against the other – a violin effect, if you will.

Now that we knew what produced this sound the next question was where did it come from. I suspected that a cricket's call would not travel through two classroom doors and across a large hallway. To find out we left our door open and awaited another round of "singing". It seemed to come from close to that door. To pinpoint the exact location I stepped gingerly out to the hall so as not to vibrate the wooden floor and alarm our visitor.

In a few moments he piped up again and I discovered his location. Close to our classroom door was a drinking fountain, and the cricket was right under the base of it.

Now, how did our guest get there? Crickets leap rather than fly so it hadn't come in through the classroom windows. With children entering and leaving the building eight times a day it probably sneaked in on one of these occasions, made its way up about seven stairsteps to our first floor level, and found himself a new home.

And what a marvelous home it was! In the wild crickets like to live under a rock or piece of wood; a place where they receive some protection from marauding predators and chilly autumn weather. What safer place than a small hole under a wooden floor with a heavy, immovable drinking fountain right overhead? As far as warmth goes our classroom was directly over the school's furnace room, so keeping warm as winter approached was no problem for him. Also, it would not take much water spilled or leaking from straight above him to supply our new resident with all the liquid he would require. Since he lived in a rather dark environment this would give him further protection from his enemies. He probably ate noseeums that moved about in his cozy little cavern. Talk about being as snug as a bug in a rug!

I once read that you can tell within a few degrees what temperature it is on a summer evening by the number of chirps a cricket makes in a minute; the warmer the weather the more chirps it puts out. I doubt if I could have tested out this theory on our cricket as he rarely made music for that long at one time.

We really enjoyed our resident cricket just outside our door and affectionately named him Jiminy, after Jiminy Cricket from the movie Pinocchio. He would chirp now and then, not at any set times, and we were greatly pleased by his musical contribution to our workplace.

I can't remember exactly when it happened, but some time around the onset of winter we realized that we had not heard Jiminy lately. My first thought was that we had become so used to his pleasant music for several weeks that maybe we were just tuning him out like background music from a radio. Surely he hadn't abandoned his cozy quarters. I then began to read up on crickets and found that our local species rarely survive over the winter as adults. As I told he class, this is likely why we were no longer hearing from Jiminy. The problem with wild creatures, you see, is that you never know just how long they will be around. While it lasted I think we were treated to what was likely a unique experience in an urban school setting in Ontario.

THE DAILY ATTENDANCE REGISTER

Many more experienced (I won't call you older) teachers will remember all too well the old blue (and later red) attendance register wherein every school day the teacher made various entries. Some time in very recent years the use of this large book was done away with, much to the delight of elementary school teachers. Instead nowadays a teacher just notifies the office of the pupil absences and/or lates and the school secretary then keeps the attendance records for the whole school via the computer.

It wasn't so easy a matter when the daily register, which was usually kept in the top drawer of the teacher's desk, had to be activated by entering certain initial information at the start of school in September. Then the teacher made the daily entries right through till the end of June, summarizing each of the ten months' attendance in turn.

On the left side of that September page the teacher had to make entries down three columns. First was the list of pupils' names, by grade, surname first. In the second column each pupil's register number was entered, some of which contained up to four digits. Why a child in school needed a register number heaven only knows. Fortunately this practice was done away with in the very early 1950s. In the third column the teacher listed the birthdate of each pupil.

Only the September page was of full width. For the remaining nine months of the school year the pages were shorter widthwise so that the three columns mentioned above did not have to be completed more than once, thank goodness. Each register contained enough pages to serve for a five year period.

Across the top of each page were printed in the dates for the school days of that month. (Finally there was something we didn't have to enter in ink.) Down the column under the date, some time in the afternoon we teachers would draw a vertical pen stroke beside the name of every pupil who was present that day. If a pupil were absent for a whole day an A was inserted. If there was an absence for a half day only, the space was divided in two by a diagonal line. Then for a morning absence an A was printed in the upper half, and for an afternoon absence it was entered in the lower half. When a pupil was late for school an L was entered in the same way. Sometimes as I was making these various entries I felt like Bob Cratchit in that Dickens classic, A Christmas Carol, slaving away under the watchful eye of Ebeneezer Scrooge. At the bottom of each daily column the totals for the day were entered, and at month's end at the right side of the double page the total monthly attendance for each pupil was inscribed. When each of these sets of figures were totaled (and they had to agree or else!) that final figure was entered in the bottom right corner of the page. Remember, in those days we had no adding machines or pocket calculators in schools to help us arrive at these totals.

Then the teacher worked out the class attendance as a percentage, correct to three decimal places, and handed that figure in to the principal, who in turn sent it on to the   inspector, who then sent it to the Department (later Ministry) of Education in Toronto. This monthly figure was necessary as government grants to school boards were based on pupil attendance. This was changed to pupil enrolment some time in the mid-1950s, and teachers were pleased with this move as it meant less bookkeeping for them at the end of each month.

It certainly paid not to enter the As and Ls beside the wrong names. I remember in that case using a liquid eraser to make corrections. After it loosened the spot of ink it was carefully blotted up and allowed to dry for a minute before writing in the correct entry for that space. When making entries in the register for the day I soon learned two important things. Do it at a quiet time when all the pupils are busy at some assignment. Also, enter first the absences and lates in their correct places, and then make the line of vertical pen strokes around those As and Ls. I have been told by teachers who retired in recent years that only the absences and lates were entered in each daily column, and thus it was no longer necessary to draw that seemingly endless line of pen strokes down the page.

Before the mid-1950s there was an added complication in entering pupil absences. Instead of merely printing in an A a teacher had to inscribe one of four letters, which I remember by the mnemonic SHOP – S for sickness, H for home help, O for other reasons, and P for parental neglect. I recall sometimes having to read between the lines of the note a pupil gave me to figure out just which one of the four letters I should enter in the register.

Up until 1961-62 there was another daily entry to be made along the bottom of each column. Two temperatures of the classroom, fifteen minutes after school started in the morning and afternoon, had to be recorded. I found this a pain to remember twice a day, and within a very short time I invented a shortcut. I had a pupil who was blessed with a good memory and who sat next to the thermometer write down the two desired temperatures each day. Then, some time during the afternoon when I was doing the register I looked over at my monitor, cleared my throat, and she would automatically respond, for example, "70 and 72" (degrees Fahrenheit).

This recording of daily temperatures was probably a holdover from earlier days when in a one-room rural school a person was hired to come to the school early to light the fire in the woodstove each morning. I think this practice of recording temperatures should have expired, at least in larger multi-roomed schools with furnaces and caretakers, long before it was laid to rest.

There were two additional pages of interest in the classroom register years ago. On the very first page was a blank chart with three headings: date, inspector's signature, and comments. Before completing his annual visit the inspector (later superintendent) filled in this information. Upon looking over several old registers in the archives at the local school board office I found the following comments to be most prevalent: satisfactory, good, very good, and excellent. One superintendent who had a sharp mind for numbers wrote comments like "Check the total for line 24." Another one wrote "Be neater, please." Just as soon as my inspector finished his visit the first thing I did was to see what his comment was. I am told by present-day teachers that this chart no longer appeared in school registers some time after my retirement in 1984. On the very last page of the register was another chart for recording the names of visitors to a classroom.

From the changes noted in this chapter you will observe that keeping the register gradually became easier to do over the last fifty some years, until finally the register itself was no longer used. I was born too soon to celebrate that blessed event.

A ROYAL CHANGE

You probably would not expect an occurrence that took place on the other side of the Atlantic Ocean would change a classroom routine in most elementary schools right across Canada. Yet that's what happened on the morning of February 6, 1952. When I came down for breakfast at the hotel where I boarded one of the other residents gave us some sad news. He had just heard on his radio that King George VI had died.

Right after breakfast I turned on my radio to get more details of the king's passing. Most people knew that in the days before his death his health had been fading rapidly and thus his departure did not come as a sudden shock. The announcer on the 8:00 A.M. news broadcast gave his listeners a brief history of the main events in his life and highlighted the king and queen's visit to Canada in May, 1939, (he was the first reigning monarch to visit our country) and how the royal couple had spent much time rallying the beleaguered people of England during the dark days of the Battle of Britain in 1940.

The newsman concluded this biography with a sentence I had never heard before. "The king is dead, long live the queen." I thought at first that this was a rather indignant remark to make about a man who, while he was perhaps not cut out to be a king, nevertheless did his best at that demanding position. I found out later that this statement was not at all meant to be offensive, that it might be paraphrased to mean, "Individuals are born and die, but may the monarchy prosper."

This sentence kept going through my mind, and on the way to school it suddenly hit me. We can no longer sing God Save the King at school but from now on we must sing God Save the Queen. Opening exercises in those days consisted of three parts: first the Lord's Prayer, followed by God Save the King, and then the daily bible reading. (In my experience teachers switched from singing the royal anthem, God Save the Queen, to our national anthem, O Canada, during the 1960s.)

After we said the Lord's Prayer that morning I told the class that the king had died during the night and since our new monarch, his daughter Princess Elizabeth, was now on the throne we should sing God save our gracious queen, rather than king. So we tried it. I gave them the starting note on the pitchpipe as usual and then said one, two, sing as I beat three-quarter time with my arm. It did not work. Five words into the anthem they said king rather than queen, and who could blame them after singing it that way every school day for the last five or six years? I stopped them right there and had them sit down. Taking a piece of chalk I wrote on the blackboard:

God save our gracious QUEEN,

Long live our noble QUEEN,

God save the QUEEN.

Send HER victorious,

Happy and glorious,

Long to reign over us,

God save the QUEEN.

I had them stand and we tried it again, only this time I pointed out each word on the blackboard with a pointer. They got it right, but would they remember that the next day?

Next morning just before we sang I asked them what we were to remember this morning. I did not ask for an answer but let them think about it for a moment. We started up, and they sang it as though the queen had been on the throne for years. The reason they were successful was probably that the subconscious part of their brains repeatedly kept telling them, "Don't forget to sing QUEEN instead of KING tomorrow."

As I reflected on this incident I thought that people in schools on that morning in 1952 had a unique experience. Since 1901 no classes in Canada had had to make the substitution between KING and QUEEN in the royal anthem. The previous gender change in the monarchy occurred in that year when Prince Edward, son of Queen Victoria, became King Edward VII.

GRADE 8 GRADUATION

Do you remember graduating from elementary school? Year after year for each grade 8 class it is a time when people about fourteen tears of age do quite a bit of wondering about their lives, both past and future. They recall no doubt the various experiences they had in their present school building from kindergarten (or J-K) through to grade 8, where they likely knew a number of the pupils in what was for most of them a smaller school setting, yet at the same time they ponder what is in store for them in grade 9 in a larger building, a different method of teaching (moving from one classroom to another on a rotary schedule), and spending the years ahead with an almost entirely new group of people.

But the winding down of elementary school days does not begin on graduation day. Just as we can't say when the first light of dawn appears, so it is with the realization that for some pupils their years in a K to 8 school are drawing to a close. But by mid-June there are positive signs that grade eighters are aware that the end is near.

I noticed this as a teacher on yard supervision. At this time of year the grade 8 pupils are not as active as they were the rest of the year. They seem to be milling about in a small area of the playground, talking to one another. Having noticed this scene over several years I suppose they had reached the time when they became aware that their elementary school days would soon be over. By now they would have counted the number of days left at their present school, and soon they would begin to count the number of hours remaining.

Today photographers usually take pictures of all classes in a school, but in my own school days and some of my earlier years of teaching it was only the grade 8s that had their photos taken, and that occurred in early June, usually at the front of the school. (Do you still have your grade 8 photo, and can you name off all those classmates without having to turn over and read their names on the back of the picture?) Here was another reminder that those eight, nine, or ten years of elementary school would soon be finished (a big chunk of a lifetime). If you visit some older schools you may see a line of grade 8 photographs mounted on a wall in the main corridor of the building.

Of course graduation day was the big event, and it occurred on the second last day of school. (There's nothing like having the last day off to lord it over the rest of the school.) In most schools a grade 8 clapout was held. All the other classes formed two lines, one on either side of the sidewalk leading up to the main doors of the building. Then the principal would let one graduate at a time walk out of the building. Just as soon as a person appeared at the doorway the clapping began, and continued until he/she reached the end of the line of pupils. Then another pupil appeared and the clapping began again. The annual clapout was a very nice way for the rest of the classes to say goodbye to the graduating pupils.

Then came the activities of graduation night. In one school I taught at they began by eating a meal, thanks to the Home and School Association, but most schools started around 8:00 P.M. with a set program. Foremost of course was the giving out of the grade 8 graduation certificates. (Do you still have yours?) This was usually done by the grade 8 teacher(s), and I remember it being a rather emotional time for some pupils. A colleague of mine, after he had presented his last certificate, turned to the audience and said, "I've never shaken so many wet hands before."

Some awards of excellence were also handed out to deserving pupils. These varied somewhat from school to school but usually included ones such as academic excellence, leading citizenship, and most improved pupil.

Naturally there would be a guest speaker, on most occasions someone in the field of education. The main gist of his or her deliverance was usually along the line of stay with it, do your best, and don't give up.

Finally came the valedictory address (literally saying goodbye), delivered by one of the top pupils among the graduates. A valedictorian at any level of education is expected to say thanks to those people who helped the graduates achieve their goal of the day.

Then suddenly graduation was over. But isn't that the way life goes? We start at the bottom of some sort of ladder and before you know it we're at the top. Then we start climbing another set of rungs, and go from one ladder to another – elementary school, high school, college or university, occupation(s), and life itself. Along the way other ladders may be experienced such as marriage, raising a family, avocations, and new challenges resulting in worthwhile accomplishments.

Remember, it isn't the final goal that's important, but how you played the game along the way.

THE WRITE WAY TO STUDY

Did they teach you how to study in elementary school? Not likely. Did they teach you how to study in secondary school? Again, not likely. Did they teach it at university or college? Fat chance. You spend a fair bit of time writing tests and examinations in institutions of learning. Doesn't it strike you as being rather odd that you were not taught how to study for them somewhere along the line?

Right up till the end of high school I didn't think much about studying. I did as most students do, just reading over my texts and notebooks. Somehow I passed every year without a lot of effort, but when I started taking university courses and the cost of them came out of my pocket, that was another kettle of fish. Since I did not want to lose that money by failing any courses I gave this matter of studying some careful thought.

The verb study has several meanings, but in relation to preparing to write an examination I think it means this. It is an attempt to put into the brain and retain there   certain knowledge that people have to reveal to a teacher, professor, etc. who require them to do so via an examination paper. Some people call this simply regurgitating information, which has an unpleasant connotation, but call it what you will, you have to write this requested knowledge down on paper in an examination room and hand it in when the allotted time is up.

So how should one prepare for exams, which are nearly always written? Certainly not just by reading. We all know how easy it is to look at words on a page and not pay any attention to them while at the same time we are thinking about what we are going to do on the weekend. And how do you know, after you have "read" this information that your brain has absorbed it?

The only sure way is to write it out and then check it with the source. Here is the study method I used at university which I credited for helping me receive decent marks. First you make a survey of the material you are trying to retain, in order to get a general   impression of it. Examples:

– the interrelation of words in a sentence (grammar)

– cause and effect (some aspects of science and history)

– working with numbers to get desired results (mathematics)

– names and locations of various features on a map (geography)

In other words what is it all about? Isn't that what we do when we start any new task?

Then you have to decide how much you can do at any one sitting. There is no sense in biting off more than you can chew. With enough practice you get to know roughly how long it takes to review a certain amount of work.

One great danger in studying is that some people try to do too much in a short time period. This is especially true the night before an exam, and it is known as cramming, which leads to confusion. After much time is spent on intensive thinking the brain just goes numb. Have you ever noticed this after an hour of trying to piece together a difficult jigsaw puzzle? When this happens it's time to take a break from studying and do something physical for awhile – cut the grass, rake the leaves, shovel snow, or take a walk. Remember, the mind can only absorb what the seat can endure.

Now let's get down to the writing. It doesn't have to be written out in full sentences. Point form and abbreviations will do. The important thing is to get down all the facts you can muster.

After that you open your text and/or notebook and figure out how well you did. Taking a red pen, put a check mark beside each fact you listed correctly. Mark an X for every error and an O for every omission. Now add up all the red marks (e.g., 28) and then the number of check marks (e.g., 23). So you had 23 right out of a possible 28 – very good! You should aim for at least 75% accuracy in this work.

Now comes the correction time. Using that red pen again make the necessary corrections and add in the omitted facts between the lines in large red letters. Give yourself a mental bawling out while you're doing this.

I taught this method to some grade 8 classes, writing out on the blackboard a sample to show them what they might have written down while they studied. This example, taken from one of their school subjects, included various errors and omissions. In later years some former pupils and some parents thanked me for teaching this method of studying. They told me it was used when they went on to high school.

The big difference between using this approach and just reading over your notes and texts is that this one involves more effort, but isn't that true of any worthwhile endeavour?

BRENDA GETS SKUNKED

Yes, unfortunately Brenda got skunked, and I don't use that word with the meaning cribbage players give it. If you play that game and your opponent(s) beat you by more than thirty points you are said to be skunked.

No, I use the term in the way that almost everyone in this part of the world knows. That small black animal with the two white stripes down its back feels that some sort of dangerous situation is encroaching upon him and to drive off anything that might harm him he lets fly with his fetid fluid.

Most of us have met up with el stinko in one of two ways. You may have left your bedroom window open at bedtime and were later awakened in the night by the reeking smell permeating through your house. Or you may have seen a dead skunk ahead of you while driving down a road. You knew that if you did not close the car windows and drive carefully around it you and your car would get skunked.

Brenda's encounter with a skunk occurred one bright October morning on her way to school. When the bell rang pupils came into the school to their classrooms as usual. Our room was located on the second floor and I customarily stood at the top of the long, steep stairway leading to it. (Some of those older schools had very high ceilings.) As Brenda passed by me I detected a certain unpleasant odour, so I asked her to step out of line and then made idle conversation with her. I wanted to get a closer whiff. Sure enough, it was skunk that I smelled.

When I asked her if she had met up with a skunk on her way to school she claimed she never saw any skunk that morning. I pondered about this for a moment and then figured out how she might have been skunked unknowingly. It had been a rather pleasant night, and the skunk was likely out looking for a meal in the dark, probably enjoying that time of year when the heat of summer was no longer a problem and he was not yet concerned about being denned up in the cold of winter. (Sounds like another animal we know, doesn't it?) After his nocturnal roving he probably holed up at dawn in or under one of the many outbuildings or verandahs in his territory. Like many school children through the years Brenda likely took a shortcut through a neighbour's property, and that's when it happened.

I should say that Brenda was not badly sprayed by the skunk, Since the perfume she wore to school that morning was only mildly offensive no doubt the skunk did not release much of his liquid defence in her direction – just enough to give her a warning. Or maybe what she passed through was the remains of an earlier bout of smelling up the area. Nevertheless she continued on to school seemingly unaware of what had happened. Perhaps this explained why, when the pupils were coming up the stairs, they did not try to keep their distance from Brenda. Then again maybe young people's olfactory organs are not yet fully developed.

I instructed Brenda to go home right then and there at the top of the stairs, take a long bath using plenty of soap, and suggested that her mother wash the clothes she was wearing at her earliest convenience. She was to return to school when she and her mother thought they had got rid of the bad odour. I am pleased to say that Brenda was back at school that afternoon, smelling like a rose. I chalked the whole thing up to just another interesting and unusual occurrence in the life of a teacher.

Speaking of skunks reminds me, have you heard what song the skunk sang when it found itself on a hill and the high wind that was blowing reversed its direction? "It All Comes Back to Me Now."

CLASS PHOTOGRAPHS

As I recall it the day the photographer came to take class pictures was one of the happier events that took place at school. While we didn't realize it at the time here was a memento that would bring back fond memories of our youthful past many years later. The photo might have been taken in June, not long before that special occasion known as the grade 8 graduation exercise or it could have been snapped at any time during your school year to serve in the future as a record of those who spent a year with you in Mr, Miss, or Mrs. _____'s class back in 19___.

Do you remember the hustle and bustle when you arrived at the front of the school or some other suitable location for the photography? The camera man was busy setting up his equipment while everyone was milling around talking about everything and nothing both at the same time. You looked at the bleachers or school steps, wondering just where you might be placed, hoping it would be near your friends or better still, next to that good-looking girl/boy who lived down the street from you.

The photographer probably determined your position in one of two ways. Either he sized up your height on the spot and, pointing to you, aimed you to move to a certain place in a particular row (usually back to front) or he said, "Line up according to height, girls on this side and boys over there." Then he could select you more easily. If it were a young group then there was the inevitable tip-toeing among the boys to prove who was taller than who. When the photographer had you all lined up and could see everyone through his camera lens he gave you the usual directions, "Look at the camera and say cheese." Two or three flashes later and it was all over.

On looking at a number of old class photos in my filing cabinet I notice that there are two main facial expressions on the pupils. Some of the people are smiling while most of them have a perfectly blank look on their faces. In a few cases the facial expressions truly reflect their owners' personalities. Some photos contain a hairbrained Harry, looking cross-eyed and with his tongue hanging out the corner of his mouth. (Look everybody, aren't I funny?) I wonder what he thinks of himself while looking at that picture years later. Then we have his opposite, grim Gus, whose facial expression is a cross between a snarl and a grimace. (I'm not going to smile at any dumb camera!) In the second row we have shy Shirley. (Is she really shy or just being coy with the photographer?) In the third row is angry Andrew, a handsome lad who is most put out because he is standing between two not so glamourous girls. Invariably there is a sleepy Sam, who just happens to blink at the wrong time. We sometimes see a frowning Fred. (How much longer must I put up with this nonsense?) Now and then we find an eccentric girl who is overdressed. In one photo I have where everyone else is wearing normal street clothing, weirdo Wilma is wearing a brilliant blue outfit dappled with large pansies that completely covers her from neck to ankles. At first glance she appears to be wearing a bathrobe! (Look world, here I am.) Occasionally one person will be caught looking up at the sky or off to one side. (Is that a bird or a plane I see?) Finally we have cute Clara, whose pose suggests she'll be a future Miss Canada. (Look for me as a pin-up queen in a few years.)

When you look at those old school photographs various thoughts come to mind. Did we really wear clothes like that when we were in school? And, having seen some of these classmates in recent years, have you noticed that some really haven't changed at all while there are others who look completely different now, so much so that without an introduction you would not know who they are? If you are ever in an older school where in the main hallway there are many class photos dating back fifty years or more see if you can guess in what decade they were taken. It really isn't that difficult if you look closely at the different hair styles and clothing that change with the passing years.

Finally, I well remember the good advice my grade 8 teacher gave us when we received our grade 8 graduation pictures. "Don't forget to write the names of your fellow classmates on the back of the picture. If you don't you won't remember in a few years who some of them are." We did not laugh at this idea, but I'm sure he knew by the looks on our faces that we didn't believe him. I have a few class photos of pupils I taught wherein I did not follow his suggestion. He was dead right. Nowadays I can't put a name to many of them.

THE STRAP

No matter what I say about this topic some feathers are bound to be ruffled, but here goes anyway. Some people claim that the strap should never have been taken out of schools while others maintain that it should have been removed years earlier. When I started teaching there was a strap in every one-room rural school and in every classroom in graded elementary schools. Today they are no longer found in any school, and present-day pupils in all likelihood have never seen one.

Looking back over the last fifty years it seems to me that western society is moving more and more in the direction that no one should be afraid, that with all our modern technology, conveniences, and discoveries we should not have to fear anything. Think about that for a moment. In the physical world if we did not have a certain degree of fear (call it respect) many of us would be dead before we were thirty years old. In crossing a city street when the traffic is heavy do we not look around carefully before stepping off the curb? Do we swing metal golf clubs around during a game of golf or go across a lake in a boat when bright flashes of lightning are illuminating the sky? And before climbing twenty feet or more up a ladder do we not check carefully to make sure the ladder is on a proper angle and that it is on solid footing? We simply cannot remove fear from our day to day living.

In the same way that we know we must pay for the grievous errors we make in the physical world, then I believe the same results should be expected in our social world. Can you imagine a society in which there is no law and order, where anyone could do whatever he wanted to without fear of reprisal or consequences? We would soon have a very chaotic world.

When the strap was used properly in the classroom it was quite effective. The offender's punishment was immediate, and it let him know that what he had done was wrong and that it was not to happen again. In my retirement years when people find out that I was a former teacher they often tell me about their elementary school days, and sometimes their experiences with the strap arise. None of them hold any grudges against the teachers who strapped them, and they claim that the disgrace of having done something wrong hurt inside far more than their temporarily stinging hands. Moreover they say that getting the strap did not leave them with lifelong psychological scars. They also tell me that they deserved to get it, and mention that they did not tell their parents about it for fear of getting more punishment at home. My how times have changed.

I recall when the strap was not used properly, and thus had little or no effect. One recess three of us teachers and the principal of a school were chatting in his office. A loud noise was suddenly heard from his adjoining classroom, so he left us to investigate. (He had a few pupils in there doing some sort of chore for him.) One minute later he marched a grade 8 lad into the office. Without saying a word he reached into his desk and removed a worn-out, frayed strap which had all the stiffness of a piece of cardboard, and within ten seconds he hastily strapped the boy twice on each hand (pat, pat, pat, pat). Then he told him to get out. I can well imagine how quickly this boy told his pals about the effectiveness of that strapping.

Over the years I've heard parents say that they would not want their children strapped because it would hurt them. Of course it would hurt. That's why it was used, and as one school psychologist once told a group of us, it worked. No one wants to see his/her child hurt unfairly, but consider this real life analogy. A mother is vacuuming a floor while her two year old son is watching. She unplugs a floor lamp already lit, lifts it out of the way, and vacuums up that area. Then she plugs the cord back in and the light comes on again. The child finds this sudden reappearance of the light quite fascinating, and starts trying to poke a small object into the electrical outlet. Now, what should the mother do – try to reason with a curious two year old? I think she should give the little fellow a couple of whacks on the behind end and say, "No!" That's what I call tough love, and it might prevent him from suffering an electric shock in the future. The strap, likewise, was a deterrent for undesirable behaviour.

Are there alternatives for the strap in schools today? A teacher can reason with some pupils to a certain extent and temporary isolation from the classroom by "solitary confinement" in the hall or the principal's office may work with others. I doubt, however, that the few incorrigibles which teachers meet up with can be changed by these methods. Suspension of a pupil is a more serious alternative, but the pupils who are suspended are usually those who most need to be in the classroom academically. Moreover, if their parents do not support the school concerning these suspended pupils then they are not likely to change their ways.

For a classroom to function properly there must be a reasonable degree of law and order. From what I hear about the lack of it in some classrooms nowadays it seems that some teachers are wasting a lot of time and energy trying to solve discipline problems. These unfortunate teachers are like a person who is constantly mopping up water running across a floor from a tap that is turned on and left running. It would be much more effective, and easier on their well-being, if these teachers could simply go to the source of the trouble and turn off the running tap. Once upon a time in our schools we had the means to turn that tap off. Today it is gone.

THE YEAR I LEARNED MORE THAN MY PUPILS

It's not difficult to guess which year in my teaching career I'm referring to in this title. I'm sure most teachers would agree with me that we learned more about teaching in that first year on the job than in any other.

Now I'm not faulting the teacher training I received in the previous year. Goodness knows we students at normal school (renamed teachers' college in the early 1950s) had plenty of practice in teaching children. From late September through to May we taught one lesson a week, half of them in one-room rural schools and the other half in city schools from kindergarten to grade 9. Also, in December and March we taught for most of a week in graded schools in the city, and in January and April in rural school settings. Maybe if I had listened more closely to what we were told in normal school about the non-teaching aspects of running a classroom I would have been better prepared for my first year on the job, but being nineteen and twenty years old my mind was on other things. (Guess what?)

That first morning of my beginning year of teaching started off on a very busy note. I was doing my best to remember during the roll-call what names belonged to what faces and trying to figure out who should sit where – not a simple problem when you have forty-seven pupils in two grades. I tried to get those with hearing and sight problems close to the blackboard and I wanted to avoid a problem we discussed at normal school – short children sitting in seats too high for them. When this occurs one of two things happens. Either their feet will swing back and forth an inch or so above the floor and in time their legs will hurt, or else they will slouch down in their seats in order to rest their feet on the floor, which in turn is not good for their backs.

By morning recess new supplies and books had been

issued, a temporary seating plan had been drawn up, and we had settled in to our new room somewhat. I gave the class their first assignment, that old opening day standard, write a paragraph telling me about your summer activities. That's when I made a sudden realization. In all my years at elementary school I sat in the same seat from 9:00 A.M. till 4:00 P.M., getting only three breaks – two recesses and the noon lunchtime. We had no library period (no library) and no physical education classes (no general purpose room). So for most school days I was desk-bound. Now that I was seated on the other side of the teacher's desk for the first time on my own I said to myself, "Why are you sitting here when your pupils are all busy at their work?" So I got up and walked down the aisles to see how they were doing. That's one of the pluses in teaching. You don't have to sit or stand for any great length of time, and you have much leeway in alternating between them.

From the back of the room I meandered over to the windows. Since my classroom was on the second storey of the building, which had been erected on higher ground, I had a good panorama of much of the village. Suddenly I recognized the old hockey arena where three and four years earlier I had played juvenile hockey. Fond memories came flooding back. Then realization #2 hit me. "Why are you here staring out the window?" I soliloquized. "You were hired to teach these children behind you. Get back to work, Paterson." That's when I truly realized that I was responsible for the outcome of my pupils at school. Since that day I never walked over to a school window to look out at anything unless it had something to do with my job.

It wasn't the actual teaching that was the problem that first year, but all the other things associated with life in a classroom. First and foremost was learning how to cope with those pupils whose personalities were so far removed from the norm that they provided me with a challenge at times. There was the matter of trying to keep the lid on the class clown, attempting to bring shy, quiet, and unnoticed pupils out of their shells, and letting a couple of trouble-makers know that I was not about to tolerate any of their nonsense.

But the greatest cause of concern was a very clever young lassie who always seemed to be one step ahead of me. Learning came to her quickly and easily, and she had her seatwork completed away ahead of the rest of the class and then found it boring with having nothing to do. With no library in the school and not even a few children's books in the classroom for pupils to read I was fearful that she would become a prime example of the devil making idle hands busy. I convinced her to bring to school some books from the village library to read whenever she completed her assignments.

During that beginning year there were some concerns that kept recurring in my mind. One was would there be enough time within the school year to complete the work in a certain subject on the curriculum? Just as bad though was the thought that maybe I would finish the course of study in a given area too soon, and then what would I do each remaining week in those periods of time? Years later this very thing happened to a first year teacher who confided in me that by late winter he had covered the Social Studies course for his grade level and was now in quite a quandary. On the other hand an experienced teacher nearing his retirement once told me, "You know, each year I seem to teach less subject matter but I think I teach it better." So quality ranks up there just as much as quantity.

Another query I had was the matter of discipline. All of us can remember some teachers who had it and some who did not. Fortunately my first class was by and large a well behaved group who did not put me to the test during year one. I suppose that over the year certain disciplinary measures gradually improved, like the dramatic pause when speaking, lowering the voice to gain attention, and the development of the "teacher's hard look" that says, "That's enough of that now, let's get back to business."

Yet another concern was trying to steer a middle course between the two extremes of being too strict or demanding with my pupils but on the other hand being too lenient with them. Finding a path midway between being too easygoing and too overpowering is something that takes a while to learn.

I found the first year of teaching to be one of much experimentation. If this doesn't work, try that, or something else. As in any venture practice improves performance.

When I finished teaching for the day then the night shift began. How well I remember those evenings when I laid out my course of studies, texts, and the few reference books I had, and began getting ready for the next day. Some of those nights seemed awfully long. Some people say that teachers work only from 9:00 till 4:00. In my first year of teaching I could have agreed with that statement, because it felt sometimes as though I had worked from 9:00 A. M. till 4:00 A.M.

The next year and thereafter things went a lot more smoothly. And what was the reason? As my grade 7 teacher often told us, "Experience is the best teacher but it costs the most."

CLASS TRIPS

There's no doubt about it, most kids love a class trip. That's probably because although the trip takes place on a school day the pupils like the fact that they are not just putting in another day in the classroom. If it is an all day bus trip they enjoy what they might consider to be a "holiday on the highway". The other nice feature of a class trip of course is the expectation of what for most of them is a new experience when they reach their destination.

Someone who has no connection with the teaching profession might think that a full day class trip is a copout for the classroom teacher. It isn't, when you consider all the organization that is involved. First there is the question of choosing a site to be visited that is related to the interest level of the class, that is not too distant in relation to their age, and that is in some way connected to what they are learning at school. In other words it is not just a picnic. With that decided contact is then made with the facility to be visited to see on what suitable date(s) they can accommodate you.

Then arrangements must be made with a bus company to provide transportation, and where and when meals are to be eaten must also be decided. With this information on hand parental consent forms have to be sent home and returned to the school by a certain date.

Somewhere along the line the matter of raising money to pay for the trip must be considered, which might involve fundraising ventures beyond school time. As the big day draws near the teacher will discuss with the class what clothing would be appropriate, depending on the time of year and the weather forecast.

When the children get off the bus at their destination a problem of much concern for the teacher may arise. Some pupils, having their physical freedom after being cooped up in the bus for some time, may see ahead any number of situations they might like to explore on their own. If there are several other classes visiting in a fairly spacious area it's easy to see how one or more pupils could become lost in the crowd of young people round about. So the teacher must act as a shepherd of the flock to prevent any of the sheep from getting lost.

Finally, in the days following the trip the teacher has to tie together the new knowledge the class has learned from the trip to their everyday work in the classroom.

You can readily see that with all this extra work the teacher is involved in concerning a class trip it would be much easier for him or her to simply teach another day back in the classroom.

The first trip I took a class on was in 1951 in my second year of teaching and it certainly didn't involve all these steps. The village of Lakefield was widely known for the fine wooden canoes and outboard motorboats made at the local boatworks. Arrangements for the trip were quite simple. As the factory was only about two blocks away from the school I stopped by there on my way home from school one day and set up the details for the visit. I then notified my principal of my intention, he gave us his blessing on the matter, and away we went on the appointed day. Parental consent for the outing wasn't even considered.

This short, simple trip had a lasting effect on one of my pupils who experienced it. At a retirement party in my honour thirty-three years later she told the group how well she had liked the visit to the boat factory, made when she was in grade 5.

When it comes to class trips for schools Peterborough's location in southern Ontario is quite enviable. To the west it's a relatively short drive to Niagara Falls and Toronto, with its wide variety of informative places. To the north it's an easy trip to the site of Ste. Marie among the Hurons and its related history. Even the drives to Ottawa and Kingston to the east are not arduous, and both have many rewarding sights.

Within a smaller radius Peterborough is also in a very favourable position for shorter class trips. Twenty miles north of the city is the boundary between the St. Lawrence Lowlands and the Canadian Shield, so here are two different geological worlds right at Peterborough's doorstep. In less than an hour's drive you go from farmland to rugged terrain consisting of granite outcroppings, myriad lakes, forests, and swampland. It is great country for people with a variety of interests in the out of doors. It is not, however, the type of terrain one should enter away from existing trails with the idea of having a pleasant jaunt. One outdoor type teacher took his class on a trip just north of the above-mentioned boundary and they became lost for a couple of hours. The lay of the land in parts of this region is such that one may easily be led astray into traveling in an undesired direction.

There were three class trips, all near Peterborough and somewhat out of the ordinary that I remember fondly. The first one was a ten mile (16km) paddle down the Otonabee River in mid-June. A week earlier my grade 8 class had a trial run on Little Lake in the heart of the city. The aim here was to teach them the basic canoeing skills, give them some practice paddling in both the bow and stern positions, and pair up a weaker paddler with a stronger one. The trip went very well, without any mishaps, and was enjoyed by all.

The next trip was undertaken by a grade 6 class on skis. Once again we had a preliminary practice held on a golf course in the city, to give pupils the feel of cross-country skis on their feet, to develop the proper glide with the skis and the use of ski-poles, and to learn how to ascend and descend the ups and downs of the land. The route was a five mile (8km) round trip a short distance north of a Kawartha lake and most of it was over ponds, marshes, and their adjoining creeks, all frozen solid and snow covered on a beautiful sunny day in early March. At noon we reached our destination, which was a mini-lake on a creek that is navigable by canoe in the warmer months of the year. I remember well how we all enjoyed eating our lunch at this pine-studded site and how pleasant it was to hear the water gurgling over a smooth, rocky area immediately upstream from us.

For a few years in the 1960s we had an outdoor education consultant who took one grade 6 class each day in September and October into an area very close to the territory where we made our ski trip. My pupils learned much on that trip about the flora and fauna of the Canadian Shield, everything from trees, wildflowers, moss, lichens, ferns, birds, amphibians, insects, and numerous creepy-crawlies. For many of them it awakened an interest in the natural environment.

There was an interesting thing I learned about taking children on trips such as these where the pupils provide their own source of movement, be it feet, skis, or canoes. For most of a class the children move as one group at an acceptable rate, but for two smaller groups you ideally need two leaders, One should be out in front holding back the gung-ho types who consider the trip to be some sort of marathon, and must "get there" at the earliest possible moment. The other small group of abnormal movers are the stragglers who always seem to be falling farther behind the rest of the class. Another leader would be helpful at the rear of this group to prod them along a little faster.

But isn't that the situation you have while teaching in any classroom? Most pupils move along through the material being learned at a normal rate, but you have a few eager beavers who are always well ahead of the pack mentally, and then you have the slower learners who need encouragement and reinforcement to keep up with the rest. What else is new?

PARENT –TEACHER INTERVIEWS

The person who first thought up the idea of parent-teacher interviews deserves a medal. While the report card prepared by the teacher sums up a child's progress and general deportment in school there is nothing that takes the place of the interview, both from the parents' and teacher's perspective. To meet one another face to face in conversation gives both parties a chance to get to know each other better, and by discussing the child's progress hopefully they can together help the child develop satisfactorily in his/her formative years. After all, they should be a team furthering the interests of the child along the road of life.

The big difference in interviews at the time I started teaching and towards the end of my career was the time of day in which they were held. As I neared retirement professional activity days were established and almost immediately parent-teacher interviews were held during school hours on one of those days each year, whereas before they were conducted on two or three consecutive evenings depending on the length of the interviews, the size of the school, and the enrolment in the classes.

The length of each interview was either ten or fifteen minutes. This was deemed to be a suitable length of time required to conduct an interview for the parents of an average child. I'm sure that many teachers will agree with me that in discussing some pupils' progress ten minutes was longer than necessary while fifteen minutes wasn't nearly long enough in other cases.

Setting up the schedule for all those interviews in a school was a Herculean task for the principal. Let's say that a parent had three children in different classrooms. The schedule was organized so that the parent could visit the three teachers concerned all on the same night, and go directly from one classroom to another. This was no mean feat to accomplish in a school with an enrolment of five to six hundred pupils and twenty teachers

To ensure that each interview did not run over its allotted time the school bell was set to ring automatically every ten or fifteen minutes on an interview evening. Knowing Murphy's law, you can guess what happened next. When the bell rang to signal the end of an interview and the teacher expected the parents to leave to make room for the next couple, sometimes the former parents still kept on talking and did not budge out of their chairs. In some cases this went on long enough that a knock would be heard on the door. It was the latter parents giving notice that according to the interview schedule posted on the door it was now time for their interview. I met up with this situation on various occasions, not only as a teacher but also as a parent of my school-age children. It took either a strong-willed or a very diplomatic teacher to get those first parents to move out. I found that in this situation the best bet was to stand up shortly after the bell rang, walk to the door and open it while still conversing, and then greet the next parents and invite them in.

Over the years there has been some debate as to the best seating arrangement for the parents and teacher during the interview. One theory has it that the teacher should be seated behind his/her desk with various information spread out on the desk top at the ready, and the parents seated facing the desk. According to these proponents this is the setup when you go to see someone in the world of business.

Those on the other side of the argument claim that this is a rather stiff arrangement, and that it does not set the parents at ease. They propose that the parents and teacher should be seated facing one another with no desk in between, claiming that this is a more informal setting.

I have used both arrangements and was quite happy with

either one, but I would defer from being an arbitrator in this matter. Since the individual teacher has to conduct all the interviews I suppose the choice should be up to him or her. Some people find that having a desk in front of them is a source of assurance; others find it an encumbrance.

Every so often a strange situation awaited me when I went to the door to greet the next parents to be interviewed. On one occasion a teenager about eighteen years old stood before me. Thinking that he was seeking help looking for someone I asked him if I could be of assistance. He then informed me that he was here for an interview concerning his younger brother, one of my pupils. So I invited him in, and when he sat down he told me a sad story. He said that his parents were just not interested in coming for an interview about their son (whom I considered to be a typically average pupil) but he thought that someone in the family should come to find out how he was doing,

I praised him for coming to the school on this occasion, told him about his brother's strengths and weaknesses, and urged him to give his brother all the moral support he could. In view of the family situation it looked like he was going to need it. Despite the unusual circumstances I thought we had a good interview.

On another occasion I met a lady at the door with her son, my pupil, in tow. Not knowing why in the world she brought the boy with her, I looked inquisitively at her and then at her son, awaiting an explanation for his presence. She informed me that since this interview was all about George then George should be with us to find out how he was doing. Suddenly I had to make a choice between two decisions. Either I could argue why George should not be in on the interview, or else concede to the mother's request. I took the view that the customer is always right. Besides, what was there to gain by getting into a spat over George's presence or absence? So we had our interview, or should I call it a watered down version thereof.

In my latter years of teaching a very pleasant situation occurred from time to time during an interview, namely that I found myself talking to one of my former pupils. This I discovered in one of two ways. First, as a Mrs. Jones came through the door and even before she took her seat she would blurt out, "I was Susan Brown when you taught me in grade 8 at Maple Ridge School." Secondly the lady or man I was interviewing did not divulge our former relationship but carried on a guessing game during the interview, to see if I would finally recognize him or her. Very occasionally I did, but more often the person sitting before me would finally reveal his or her identity. The fact that I did not recognize a former pupil should not really be surprising when you consider how much people's appearances change from their early teens to their thirties and forties.

Whenever I had this experience the tone of the interview became much more informal. I could no longer refer to the lady as Mrs. Jones, but for the rest of the time I called her Susan. Moreover I found it difficult to keep on the topic at hand, namely her child, but instead I wanted to talk about the good times we shared years earlier back in the classroom. These situations made me aware of the fact that I wasn't getting any younger, and always reminded me of a conversation that took place many years before. A few of us teachers were chatting one recess when we were joined by the board's music supervisor who was with us for the morning. She informed us, "Well, here we go again. Another child just finished telling me that I taught her mother. I must be getting older than I thought." With that an elderly spinster on staff who was very close to retirement interjected, "Huh, you think you're getting old. Wait till you start teaching their grandchildren!"

A VERY SAD DAY

Not all relations between a teacher and his or her pupils are happy or humourous. In fact sometimes quite the opposite is true. Such was the case in my second year of teaching when a terrible tragedy took place in the community.

A pupil named Ron in my grade 5 class, aged 11,and his 13 year old brother broke into a local hardware store one night and stole two 22 rifles and some ammunition. It wasn't too difficult for them to gain entry into the store as it was being renovated and part of an outside wall was not overly burglar-proof as it was covered somehow with tarpaulins. Thus began a very bizarre incident on a weekend in late May.

The boys told their father on Sunday afternoon that they were going to the river to do some fishing. Actually this was just a ruse. Their real intention was to go to the local quarry to do some shooting with their newly acquired firearms. The quarry was at the edge of the village, fairly near their home, and was by then abandoned as the former cement company that had procured limestone from it left the village in 1932.

I said the boys intended to use the quarry as their site for firing their recently acquired guns, but they did not go there to shoot at specified targets around the walls of the quarry. What they had in mind was to pretend that they were back in the lawless days of the wild west in a shootout between let us say Wyatt Earp and his posse of good guys and Jesse James and his train robbers. In short they were about to shoot at each other! One wonders whether they were even aware of the terrible danger they held in their hands.

Within the quarry there were various hummocks and knolls which offered some measure of protection from the gunfire from each of the brothers. When they had selected their respective "foxholes" their game of cops and robbers began.

Now the quarry was close enough to the village that the sound of their guns going off could be heard by the people living near the former cement works. It just so happened that two of Ron's classmates out walking heard the noise, went to investigate it, and when they recognized the two doing the shooting they vehemently urged them to stop, telling them how dangerous their exchange of bullets was. But it was to no avail. A fateful conclusion was about to occur.

At this point you could almost guess what was going to happen. With shot after shot being exchanged by the boys playing out their fantasy, you would expect that sooner or later one of them would be hit. How long the shooting continued no one knows, but at one point Ron raised his head over his protective cover, and that's when a bullet caught him in the temple. His brother ran for help, and soon a doctor drove at a dizzying speed over the rough road into the site. As he was driving down the highway to the hospital in Peterborough poor Ron died.

You might wonder what would possess two young boys to undertake such a foolhardy venture as this. Perhaps some family history could answer that question. The two boys grew up in a very poor family. At the time of this calamity they were living with their father. The mother was not residing in the home then. Why, I don't know, although she did attend the funeral. One of the pall-bearers at Ron's funeral claimed that the boys lived a very meager life. He well remembers them walking around the village in the summertime without any shoes on their feet. He also said that both boys were avid readers of books about the wild west era in the United States. These facts, along with the relative ease of procuring weapons and ammunition, led to Ron's untimely demise.

I remember Ron as a very quiet, shy boy while his older brother was rather outgoing. It was the feeling around the village that Ron followed his brother's lead in this tragic chain of events.

Within the week the school principal, caretaker, and I went to the quarry one evening to see for ourselves the layout of this unfortunate incident. We noted that the older brother had by far a better barrier for protection than Ron had, in his more exposed position. Our caretaker, a former soldier in World War II, said that Ron did not stand a chance.

The news of Ron's death had far-reaching results. Very shortly thereafter I received a call from a reporter working for the now defunct Toronto Telegram . He asked if I could provide him with a photograph of Ron to accompany his writeup of the tragedy. I sent him a class photo and indicated Ron's position therein. When he mailed me back my class picture he was good enough to include with it his article and the photo he had singled out from the class picture.

The funeral took place on the Wednesday after Ron's death, and the whole class was in attendance at a small local church that afternoon. Six of Ron's classmates acted as pall-bearers. As you might imagine with a misfortune such as this occurring in a village there were many people at the funeral. It was a very somber, emotional, and teary-eyed service that afternoon.

DÉJÀ VU

One of the joys of being a retired teacher is to meet and talk with former pupils again. This happens on the street, in stores, on the job, at events around town, and sometimes in places where you would least expect to meet them. I met one paddling his canoe on a long, serpentine creek on his way to a hunt camp and another out fishing with her husband on a remote northern lake.

They come from all walks of life and work in a variety of situations: mailmen, store clerks, city employees, clergymen, several who became teachers, secretaries, some who run their own businesses, sales people, housewives, and one who has been my barber for a number of years, just to name a few.

When I come upon them face to face they usually recognize me before I realize who they are. After all, they have changed a great deal in the twenty-five to almost sixty years since I last saw them, when they were twelve to fifteen years old. I apologize for not recognizing them right off, and then give them my standard explanation, "If I don't see people every three weeks I forget who they are."

It is a great joy to me when some individuals who gave me a bit of trouble in the classroom come over to me and introduce themselves while extending their right arms for a handshake. Whenever I meet one of these fellows and have a pleasant chat with him I am reminded of the parable of the lost sheep. Then I say to myself joyously, "Another lost sheep has returned to the fold."

I meet some of my ex-pupils at a local arena where I skate with a seniors group, and to skate with these people one has to be at least fifty years old. I find it hard to believe that I supervised them at various rinks in the area when they were back in elementary school. At times like these I truly realize I'm getting well along on the road of life.

When I taught grammar to grade 7 and 8 pupils I had them memorize the list of twenty-three auxiliary verbs. This helped them in their analysis of sentences and they found it easy to learn them as they could be rhymed off in a sort of singsong in about ten seconds. Half-jokingly I would tell them that if I met them after I retired I expected they would be able to spiel them right off to me. To this day most of my former pupils can go through that list like an auctioneer in action, and it's not just the brighter ones who can do it. One lad, who was a reluctant learner in school, saw me on the street, went out of his way to meet me, and introduced himself. Then he said, "Listen to this," and he raced through those verbs as if he had learned them just yesterday. I tell my former pupils, if only I had taught everything else that well!

How very pleasant it is to meet my former pupils and talk about our school days of yesteryear and their present lives. Just as we part from one another I thank them for still recognizing me. When they reply that I haven't changed a bit I am truly flattered.

SCHOOL REUNIONS

The aims of a school reunion are twofold. One purpose is to renew old acquaintances and the other is to bring back memories of the years when you attended that school. If you've ever been to one even before you reach the door of your old alma mater the memories start flooding back – the friends you used to walk to school with, the various activities that took place in the schoolyard, and that joyous feeling of freedom at the end of the school day when you walked out through the school door into your own world again.

Once you reenter you former institution of learning, perhaps after several years of being away from it, someone seated just inside the front door prints out your name on a piece of paper which you append to your clothing. These name tags will prove to be very helpful as you wend your way through the building.

As you meander down the main hall of the school you are struck by the fact that this passageway seems much smaller than it was years ago when you attended this school. Is this the result of some optical illusion or is it because you were much shorter back then in your school years?

Then you wander in and out of various classrooms, each one bringing to mind poignant memories of days gone by – events and incidents peculiar to each particular room, trying to remember just where you sat in the different classrooms, and of course you recall the teachers who taught you in the various rooms. With all these memories returning to you as you go from room to room you get the momentary feeling that you're reliving those school days over again.

All the while you are strolling through the school you meet others doing the same, and you wonder if you should know them from years past. Some you recognize right away because they haven't changed a bit, while others look completely different from when you last saw them. With these people it's a case of getting close enough to them to read their name tags. Because your eyes are a bit less discerning now with the passing years you wish fervently that these name tags were at least three times larger than they actually were. Isn't it amazing how some people's facial features remain the same seemingly forever while in others their countenances have changed completely with the passage of time?

Meanwhile small clusters of people start forming throughout the building as they meet others who attended the school in the same era. Then it's catchup time in the news department, and questions abound. Where are you living? What are you doing for excitement? How is your health? Sometimes it's dangerous to ask this last one. Instead of the usual, "I'm doing very well, thank you" the reply might turn into a five minute, drawn out, and no details spared litany of someone's ills, aches, operations, and anxieties. When you finally move on to another room you wished you'd never asked that question. By and large, however, most conversations at a reunion are very pleasant and they often revive memories of your former school days which have been dormant for years.

Over the years I've attended a number of reunions at schools I was associated with, most of them being an important anniversary e.g., 25th, 50th, or 100th, of some institution. Some stand out in particular.

The first was the one hundredth anniversary of Queen Alexandra, the ten room public school I attended from kindergarten to grade 8, in the city of Peterborough. Early in 1989 a committee of nine people got together and planned a two day celebration for this occasion in May.

The highlight of this reunion was the large collection of memorabilia that was displayed in the kindergarten room, which was filled with tables covered with a wide variety of items supplied by former pupils. Many people spent much time poring over everything from kindergarten artwork made in the 1930s to report cards issued in the 1940s and 1950s.

The names of all the teachers who taught in Queen Alexandra School classrooms, and the years they taught there, were posted on the each classroom door. This information was obtained from old class registers which are presently stored in the archives of the local board of education.

Some pupils were borrowed from a nearby elementary school to put on a performance. On the first day of the reunion seventy-three grade 4, 5, and 6 pupils from this school took part in an old-fashioned maypole dance, much to the delight of the audience, most of whom found it to be a new experience to them.

Six antique school desks which some readers will remember being screwnailed to the floor in rows were brought into an empty classroom. Six pupils enacted a script written for the occasion about a typical morning in Queen Alexandra School in the 1930s. One of the committee members video-taped it so that it ran continuously during the two days of the reunion.

The most grandiose reunion I attended was the one celebrating the 175th anniversary of the Peterborough Collegiate and Vocational School held in 2002. It continued for three days and must have taken a great deal of planning, especially trying to contact hundreds of alumni. The present building, opened in 1908 is obviously not 175 years old, but adding in its predecessors it has reached that venerable age as an educational institution.

Any hopes of meeting former classmates by chance while wandering around in a large building would be mighty slim. The planning committee foresaw this problem and set aside a few classrooms on the main floor of the school as decade rooms. Their doors were labelled 1920s, 1930s, etc. up to the 1990s. With this setup you could stroll at leisure reminiscing from room to room and every now and then come back to check up on new faces in your decades "chat room". I was delighted to meet many former students from my generation at P.C.V.S., some of whom I hadn't seen in over fifty years.

One classmate should have received a prize for the alumnus who came the greatest distance to attend the reunion. He was living in Costa Rica at the time and came all the way from Central America for this occasion. Talk about loyalty to the old school!

A highlight of the reunion was the effort put into it by the students attending P. C. V. S. that year, especially in the areas of art, music, and drama. The reunion closed on the evening of the third day with an excellent gala in the school auditorium. The various performances by different groups were much appreciated by the alumni present.

When the former Grove School in the south end of Peterborough celebrated its fiftieth anniversary a grade 8 class I taught there decided to hold a class reunion within the school reunion. A committee from those graduates reserved their former classroom for two hours, contacted almost all their classmates, and invited me to come along also. I was flattered.

Twenty-nine pupils from that class of 1958-59 attended that mini-reunion, and we all had a wonderful time together. Many laughs were shared, photos were taken, and numerous memories of the happy times we had that year were relived. I've talked with a few of them in recent years and they tell me there's a good chance we might have another class reunion in the near future.

The final reunion I would like to mention is an ongoing one. The graduating class of Peterborough Normal School, 1948-49, held its first reunion in the September of our first year of teaching. The next one, however, did not take place till 1994, forty-five years later! Since then we've made up for that drought by meeting every year up till now and we hope to continue on with this tradition. Father time has taken his toll on our numbers but we carry on the best we can. In the year 2009 we shall celebrate our sixtieth anniversary. If you think that's noteworthy, consider this. I read in the latest edition of a retired teachers' magazine (January 2009) of a planned reunion for a group of teachers who graduated from a normal school in 1938-39. That means they would be very close to ninety years old. It's never too late to celebrate a reunion.

Reunions concerning you don't usually come along very often. If one does, get out of that rocking chair and attend it!

WEIRD ONES

Here is a list of boners that I accumulated during my teaching years. Most of them were obtained from the multitudinous readings that teachers have to do, especially test papers. I hope you get a chuckle out of them.

1. The English scalded the cliffs to get to the Plains of Abraham.

2. Hard water is ice. It is caused by cold weather.

3. You put insulation between widows in your home.

4. An example of a parable is the Serpent on the Mound.

5. The cartridge in my knee hasn't healed yet.

6. Cold germs are so small they cannot be seen through a telescope.

7. Governor Simcoe started a navel base at York.

8. The three parts of a tooth are the front, back, and sides of a tooth.

9. The sun divides the world into Jones.

10. The harmonica scale had an accidental in it.

11. A normal student tried to teach a music lesson on three part sining.

12. The Possessive Conservatives won the last election.

13. The earthworm is important to the farmer because they are good for fishing.

14. When the moon is decreasing it is said to be wailing.

15. Cromwell demolished parliament.

16. Cyprus clouds are very high in the sky.

17. In grammar the term number is the figure in front of a question identifying a question.

18. The salutation was poor in towns during the Industrial Revolution.

19. One kind of cardboard is known as carbonated cardboard.

20. Universal suffrage is the pain going on throughout the world.

21. The author keeps you in expense most of the time.

22. The province of Newfoundland has many cold frogs.

23. What kind of adjective is English? English is an adjective that comes from England.

24. These men were called circuit riders because they went around preaching in circles.

25. The Prostitutional (Constitutional) Act was signed in 1791.

26. A frog has bugle eyes.

27. Although Silver Chief was a savage dog, once he got used to his master he would never dessert him.

28. During the buffalo hunt the women were taught how to make buffalo dung.

29. Why did Jesus die on Good Friday? The next day was the Jewish Sabbath and no one could die on that day.

30. The prevailing winds of the Bahamas are hurricanes.

31. Alexander Mackenzie introduced the secret ballet into Canada.

32. In 1800 York, or Toronto, had no schools, inns, or churches but only shrewd log houses.

33. Fish provide food for people and also monuments in their homes.

34. A fingerling is a fish with a head and a tail.

35. Sacket's Harbour was where goods were loaded and sacks of wheat were taken.

36. The word people is singular. Its plural is more people.

37. The British soldiers held the slop at Queenston Heights.

38. The custom which the natives had that is strange to us is the husbands bought their wives instead of going together for pleasure.

39. A subjective complexion refers to the bare subject.

40. San Francisco is a disturbing centre for the Central Valley.

41. Brock was killed in the champagne at Niagara.

42. The purpose of the Act of Union was to pass laws so no one would get riled up and do something.

43. Conservation is the wise use of natural resorts.

44. A fog is a stratus cloud that comes down in lawyers.

45. In pioneer times the "front" was the edge of the water.

46. The Forest Indians had very few wooden bowels.

47. An umiak is a broad boat.

48. The Indians scalloped their enemies.

49. The value of brushing your teeth before breakfast is you can put a slippery coating on your teeth so most of the food doesn't get trapped between your teeth, but slides off.

50. Tell two things that happen in an object when it is heated. – It gets warm.

51. General Brock was tall, brave, and offensive.

52. The Indians buried Tecumseh secretly and he has never been found since.

53. At this time, his wife was expecting her first child and this doubled the pressure on Lord Elgin.

54. Write one sentence about each of the following to show that you know how the Indians used it, or what it was for. – Cedar bark is the bark off the cedar tree.

55. The plural of solo is duet.

56. Car wheels nowadays have no spooks.

57. The Quakers did no want to pay taxis.

58. Keon of the Leafs intersected the puck.

59. I am going to tell you my ways of living. First it started off when I was born.

60. Madeline de Vercheres has a prominent place in our history because she was a fourteen year ago girl.

61. Wolfe defeated Montcalm on the Plains of Arabia.

62. Some Indians jumped Laura Secord near Beaver Dams.

63. The Constitutional Act allowed people to keep their own laws, religion, language, and costumes.

64. Definition of prostrate – lying with face to the ground in humidity.

65. Some chapters in this book (about health) tell you how to keep yourself clean and sweat-smelling.

66. A report card self-comment – Brian is easily disrumped by those around him.

67. A test on decimals was entitled Math. Dismals by one boy.

68. Champlain began a club known as the Legion of Good Cheer.

69. A measure (in music) is the distance between two bare lines.

70. A decimal is a fraction with an understanding denominator.

71. The opposite of longitude is shortitude.

72. In music middle c is on the leisure line.

73. Seed producing plants are found anywhere on earth except in frozen desserts.

74. Some of the United Empire Loyalists settled in the Merry Time Provinces.

ROLLING RHONDA AROUND

The sudden surge in school population due to the baby boom era brought about much better facilities in physical education during the winter months. Until that time all rooms of any size in nearly every school were strictly classrooms where "the three R's" were taught. But when all those baby boomers entered the picture either many new schools were soon built or additions were added on to older ones. Along with all these new classrooms another type of room became a mainstay of every school. The general purpose room, as its name suggests, has various uses: school assemblies, parent-teacher organizations, concerts, literary contests, graduation exercises, community events, and of course, physical education. Until a school had a GP room the physical education program suffered greatly during the winter as there wasn't much opportunity for the vigorous physical movement of young people in a room filled with thirty-odd tables and chairs.

After thirteen years of teaching I finally arrived at a school with a GP room, and was most anxious to put it to use for the winter physical education program. In it of course I used the typical elements of all my Phys. Ed. classes, namely an initial warmup jog, various exercises, a new individual stunt, review of a game skill, and then a game. Moreover that year I was looking forward to getting pupils involved in basketball and volleyball.

For a short while during that winter I took the class through various somersaults, rolls, and the like. There was nothing new about teaching these gymnastics, but my approach was different. I divided the class into five teams with six pupils per team and told them that they were allowed to help others on their team who were experiencing difficulties. This setup worked quite well as no one in the class had any major trouble completing their gymnastics, except Rhonda.

Rhonda was one of those rare individuals a teacher meets up with who has very limited athletic ability. This was not due to any infirmities or congenital defects on her part. She just didn't have any getup and go. While she was far from being thin she wasn't obese either. Perhaps a fair assessment of her avoirdupois would be pleasantly plump. Rhonda walked rather slowly in a pigeon-toed fashion. In fact, all her movements were sluggish. I realized before she started that any form of gymnastics would be an enormous challenge for her.

The class seemed to enjoy working in teams, each group assigned to its own mats and section of the GP room. The rest of Rhonda's team soon found out that she needed help, lots of it. So the other five quickly went through their routines and then devoted all their attention in coming to Rhonda's aid.

It was quite a sight to see the five teammates go to work at moving Rhonda through her various callisthenics: a push here, a pull there, repositioning themselves to get a better grip on some new part of Rhonda's physique. It was probably the first time since babyhood that Rhonda had found herself in a rolled up, head down position. All the while her team was pulling and shoving her through the motions of even a simple somersault she kept up a continual grunting and groaning reaction. She wasn't the only one making weird noises as her cohorts were echoing her sentiments as they struggled and strained to maneuver her through her gymnastic gyrations. Poor Rhonda gave them about as much co-operation as one would receive trying to get a sack of potatoes or a one hundred pound bag of sugar to make a roll or a somersault.

Now what was the reaction from the rest of the class on all this business of rolling Rhonda around? At first they were quite amused, and I couldn't blame them as it was a comical as well as an unusual sight to see. Some of them wanted to help Rhonda, but I declined their offer, telling them it was up to Rhonda's team to help her out. Besides, after the five teammates positioned themselves all around her there was no room for any more helpers.

My own reaction was that I was very pleased at the way Rhonda's helpers worked as a team to assist her. When you think about it, learning in school is a solitary business in nearly all subjects in the curriculum. Pupils don't help each other in arithmetic, history, geography, science, and most aspects of language. Two exceptions I can think of offhand are pupils acting out a play and a choir in a school performance. The rural school Christmas concert of bygone days was an excellent example of pupils helping one another in their presentation to the local community. In physical education, however, there is plenty of opportunity for pupils to aid each other in the learning process, especially in team sports.

After Rhonda left grade 8 I met her on a few occasions. Despite her physical limitations I had always found her to be a very pleasant person, and we enjoyed talking about old times back in the classroom. Whenever I mentioned the word gymnastics she would blush and chuckle about it, good sport that she was. I never asked her what line of work she went into, but you could bet your bottom dollar that it did not involve physical dexterity.

LEARNING THOSE TIMES TABLES

Do you remember in your elementary school years the stress that was put on mastering (or trying to master) your multiplication tables? Many of our parents felt that if you learned successfully the addition and multiplication facts you were half way home in the subject of arithmetic. They probably were not far from wrong because people who hadn't mastered their number facts had two strikes against them when it came to handling figures. Today with the accessibility of pocket-sized, lightweight, and cheap adding machines there is no longer the same need that existed fifty and more years ago to learn the number facts. I can still picture in my mind the clerks at the corner grocery store adding up by hand on an itemized bill the total price of various items my mother bought in the 1930s.

Can you recall how you were taught your times tables? I certainly can't. I think it was something like the process of osmosis. You leaned them so gradually and with such unnoticeable change over the years that by the time you left grade 8 they were somehow completely instilled in you (or were they)?

I suppose one of the first things a teacher has to do to help pupils learn their number facts is to convince them that it isn't the insurmountable task it appears to be. I began by asking them if they had ever sat down to learn their telephone number or street address. Since the obvious answer was no, then why was it that they knew them so well? I led them to the conclusion that first of all they really wanted to know this information (motivation) and secondly that they had seen and heard them so many times (repetition).

I next showed them, by giving each of them a copy of the following table, that there were not that many combinations to memorize.

$\frac{2}{2}$	$\frac{3}{2}$	$\frac{4}{2}$	$\frac{5}{2}$	$\frac{6}{2}$	$\frac{7}{2}$	$\frac{8}{2}$	$\frac{9}{2}$
4	6	8	10	12	14	16	18

$\frac{2}{3}$	$\frac{3}{3}$	$\frac{4}{3}$	$\frac{5}{3}$	$\frac{6}{3}$	$\frac{7}{3}$	$\frac{8}{3}$	$\frac{9}{3}$
6	9	12	15	18	21	24	27

$\frac{2}{4}$	$\frac{3}{4}$	$\frac{4}{4}$	$\frac{5}{4}$	$\frac{6}{4}$	$\frac{7}{4}$	$\frac{8}{4}$	$\frac{9}{4}$
8	12	16	20	24	28	32	36

$\frac{2}{5}$	$\frac{3}{5}$	$\frac{4}{5}$	$\frac{5}{5}$	$\frac{6}{5}$	$\frac{7}{5}$	$\frac{8}{5}$	$\frac{9}{5}$
10	15	20	25	30	35	40	45

$\frac{2}{6}$	$\frac{3}{6}$	$\frac{4}{6}$	$\frac{5}{6}$	$\frac{6}{6}$	$\frac{7}{6}$	$\frac{8}{6}$	$\frac{9}{6}$
12	18	24	30	36	42	48	54

$\frac{2}{7}$	$\frac{3}{7}$	$\frac{4}{7}$	$\frac{5}{7}$	$\frac{6}{7}$	$\frac{7}{7}$	$\frac{8}{7}$	$\frac{9}{7}$
14	21	28	35	42	49	56	63

$\frac{2}{8}$	$\frac{3}{8}$	$\frac{4}{8}$	$\frac{5}{8}$	$\frac{6}{8}$	$\frac{7}{8}$	$\frac{8}{8}$	$\frac{9}{8}$
16	24	32	40	48	56	64	72

$\frac{2}{9}$	$\frac{3}{9}$	$\frac{4}{9}$	$\frac{5}{9}$	$\frac{6}{9}$	$\frac{7}{9}$	$\frac{8}{9}$	$\frac{9}{9}$
18	27	36	45	54	63	72	81

There are 64 combinations in the above table. If you subtract the eight doubles (2 x 2 to 9 x 9) that leaves 56. Each one above the double lines is also found below these lines e.g., 7 x 5 = 35 and 5 x 7 = 35. By dividing 56 in half plus the 8 doubles, that means there are only 36 combinations to learn – truly not a gigantic task.

Then I gave them this method of trying to learn them. Taking one table at a time copy it out on paper:

2	3	4	
6	6	6	etc.
12	18	24	

Now take one combination at a time. Place your hands palms down on the desk, raise your fingers slightly, then whisper each combination ten times lowering a finger to the desk each time you say it. – six 2s are twelve, six 2s are twelve, etc. Then write out that combination ten times.

When you've gone through that complete table, take a break. Look out the window, close your eyes, or think of something else for a minute or so.

Then write out the table in a scrambled order.

8	3	6	4	9	2	7	5
6	6	6	6	6	6	6	6

Now write in the answers as fast as you can go, never minding the quality of your handwriting.

Check the answers with the original printed copy. If you had any wrong, or if you hesitated writing down an answer for even a split second, put a big fat X beside it, give yourself a mental bawling out, and write out the wrong ones another ten times. If you had more than two wrong your studying was not intense enough. In which case repeat the above steps another day.

The pupils practised this method for short periods over the course of a week, and I think it worked well because it involved an audio, visual, and tactile approach. I should add that the same method could also be used to learn the 36 addition facts. The keys to success of course were self-motivation and repetition.

In order for pupils to get further practice in mastering the multiplication tables I had a set of flash cards made, approximately five by three inches from Bristol board, and plasticized them to ensure longevity. On one side of the cards, sixty-four in all, appeared a combination (6 x 7) and on the back was the answer (42). When the afternoon dismissal bell rang I held up this set of cards, and the first person who raised a hand took them home overnight and returned them the next day. The parent, sitting on one side of a table, would hold up each card in succession, while the child across from him or her said the answer, and the parent would immediately confirm whether it was correct or not. By using this device both parent and child would readily see how well the tables were being learned.

When I met one of my former high school math teachers during my first year of teaching I asked him, "What should I be teaching my pupils in arithmetic to get them ready for secondary school mathematics?" Without any hesitation he shot right back, "Teach them to know the difference between 8 x 8 and 7 x 9."

Right on! Those fundamentals again.

YOU TEACH THEM, YOU LOOK AFTER THEM

Many of you will recall I'm sure that big transition when you went from having one teacher in grade 8 all day to having a different teacher every three-quarters of an hour or so in secondary school. If you had a grade 8 teacher who was a disciplinarian from the old school and then had some teachers in high school who were lax disciplinarians, that could be quite a shock to your system. Conversely, if your elementary school teachers let you "get away with murder" and then you found yourself confronted by no-nonsense secondary school types, that too would involve some adjustment on your part to get used to their ways. Isn't it amazing how fast students learn just what they can and can't get away with when they have a new teacher?

I never heard of a high school teacher going to another, home room teacher to get help with a discipline problem he/she was having with one or more students. I suppose at the secondary school level teachers worked under the unwritten rule "If I teach them, then I also must look after any discipline difficulties that arise concerning them." Such was not the case in my experience at the elementary school level.

In one grade 8 class I taught, the pupils had to walk three-quarters of a mile due north one afternoon a week, the girls for Home Economics and the boys for Industrial Arts. In the winter it was a chilly trip for the girls because up until the 1960s school girls (and also female teachers) wore either dresses or skirts, but not slacks.

Clothing styles do change over the years. When I attended elementary school boys wore shorts to grade 6 and after that it was long pants. Nowadays I have seen boys walking into high schools wearing shorts, in March!

But I digress. One very cold afternoon in January my class

had gone for their weekly Home Economics and Industrial Arts classes. I was on my own for the rest of the day, or so I thought. About twenty minutes after the bell rang to signal the afternoon assembly, into the classroom marched all my girls, all wearing slacks!

I immediately asked them what was up, and one of the more intrepid ones announced that their teacher had sent them back because they were improperly attired for a Home Economics class.

Now what was I to do with half a class for which I was totally unprepared and, quite frankly, rather taken aback by their sudden appearance? Perhaps the Home Ec. teacher thought I would give them a dressing down (no pun intended) on what was suitable attire for young ladies to wear to school. I don't know because she never contacted me about this matter. Maybe she figured I knew all too well that the social mores of the day dictated that girls were not to wear slacks in school, and that was that. I did not take sides in this issue with either the Home Economics teacher or the girls. I felt that time would solve the problem, and it did.

I can't recall how I occupied the girls' time that afternoon till the dismissal bell. Probably they had a long reading period. I wondered afterwards if the Home Ec. teacher thought about, or even cared about, what I was to do with half a class for two hours. Mind you, she obviously wanted to give the girls a strong message about proper school apparel, and her course of action that afternoon may have been her only feasible alternative. It was effective, as there were no more slacks worn to school that year.

While driving home that afternoon I pondered just how this situation had come about. Probably two of three of the more daring girls in the class were the ringleaders in this venture, and talked the other girls into going along with them. Whether they were truly concerned about the cold walk or wanted to show their rebellious nature, I'll never know. I do know this, however –

such an occurrence regarding girls wearing slacks to school couldn't happen nowadays.

Two years later in a different part of town, one of my grade 8 boys named Bill was sent back to me by the Industrial Arts teacher at another school. This happened on two occasions well on in the school year. Moreover, he never contacted me to say why he was sending him back to his home school. There were a couple of other lads in my class that year whom I thought were more deserving of this fate, but not Bill.

At all times I found Bill to be a pleasant boy who made quite acceptable progress in his grade 8 year. He was very likeable, quiet by nature, and got along very well with everyone I knew (except his Industrial Arts teacher). He never caused me any problem whatsoever. About ten years later our paths crossed downtown one day. Bill went out of his way to cross the street, shake hands with me, and converse for a while.

For some reason Bill and his shop teacher just didn't get along. As the school year was nearly over I realized that time would solve Bill's problem with this teacher. After his returns from Industrial Arts class Bill had a long library period for the rest of the afternoon.

For three years we had a part-time rotary system among the grade 6, 7, and 8 classes in another school. This was instigated by a principal who emulated high school procedures, and it worked quite well, giving teachers with extra skills and knowledge in certain areas an opportunity to make more use of them, and thus providing pupils with better instruction in their specialty subjects.

At this juncture you can almost guess, from the title of this chapter, just what I am about to say. One of the rotary teachers approached me one day to tell me that she was having disciplinary problems with a boy from my class, and would I have a talk with him to straighten him out.

This lady was not new to teaching, and she had taught pupils in the higher grades of elementary school for a few years. Had she been new to teaching I would have been sympathetic with her situation but at this stage of her career she should have learned how to handle a rambunctious boy. I gave her a "you teach them, you look after them" answer, and said that if one of her pupils misbehaved in my room I would not go to ask her to straighten him out.

It may seem that I dealt unfairly with this teacher, but let's look at what sort of boy it was who was out of line with her. All the time I taught Jack he was not a behaviour problem for me. I couldn't recall ever giving him even the mildest reprimand. He was an average pupil academically, well liked by his peers, and a happy, friendly person with plenty of energy to burn in the classroom. Had he been an out and out hellion I would have taken a different course of action in this matter.

The long and short of it is, in teaching you have to be your own disciplinarian. You can't expect others to deal with your problem pupils. It's too bad we didn't learn more in our teacher training about how to achieve a harmonious tone in the classroom, and thus help us to eliminate discipline problems.

GOOD TIMES

By the term good times I mean those activities which school children enjoyed in relation to memorable days of the year. The three days I concentrated upon when I taught school were hallowe'en, Christmas, and valentines day. Naturally the party on each of these days was the big event but I'm sure you all remember other happenings that took place in school leading up to these special days.

For instance in the days before hallowe'en the art lessons consisted of eerie scenes containing witches, ghosts, graveyards, and other spooky things. Traditional black and orange were the predominant colours at that time, and cutouts of cats, pumpkins, and the like adorned both the walls and windows of the classroom to help develop the proper atmosphere for October 31.

For hallowe'en music there were some excellent songs in some of those old music books at school, and as you might expect they were written in a minor key to add a haunting flavour to the melodies. When I could get hold of it I played a record entitled Danse Macabre which summed up the spirit of hallowe'en better than anything I can think of. It's about a number of skeletons coming out of a graveyard at midnight and dancing around. Sometimes the music is smooth, majestic, and flowing, while at other times the notes are quite short and jerky to suggest contrasting moods in the dance. These effects are very skilfully produced by violinists. If you close your eyes while listening to the music it's quite easy to visualize the skeletons going through their gyrations. Near the end of this record the dancing reaches a climax and the action becomes frenzied. Suddenly a rooster is heard signaling the dawn, and the skeletons all slink back to their graves. During the party I played this as appropriate mood-setting music.

In a literature period on the afternoon of the party I read to the class Ichabod Crane's Ride. Perhaps you will recall how Ichabod, rejected by the young lady he was trying to win, was riding home on his horse on a deserted road on a dark night. He met a large man who appeared to be headless, and he was carrying that head on the pommel of his saddle. (At this point I turned off the classroom lights and kept on reading.) After several vain attempts to elude his horrible pursuer that dreadful creature rose in his stirrups and hurled his head (a pumpkin) at Ichabod. At this moment I reached under my desk, drew up a paper bag stuffed full of newspapers, and threw it at a predetermined boy who hadn't seemed to be caught up in the mood of the story. The reaction each year I did this was always the same – first surprise and a few gasps and then laughter. After all pupils don't expect a teacher to do this sort of thing.

Then the party started and pastimes with apples were the order of the day. One was trying to bite into an apple tied to a string which in turn was tied to a long rope reaching across the width of the room and suspended at a desirable height. The standing contestants had to keep their hands together behind their backs while trying to sink their teeth into the apples. They soon found out that the way to do this was to trap the apple between the lips and shoulder, and then take a bite. When each one succeeded the apple was cut loose and they could eat it.

The other trick was called apple bobbing. Here a large tub was partially filled with water and apples were floated on the surface. The bobber had to push the apple to the bottom of the tub with his mouth, bite the apple, and then retrieve it out of the tub with his teeth. Needless to say it was a very wet undertaking and we had to be sure that each bobber's head and hair were completely dried before dismissal time. Both of these activities kept the non-participants well amused while they were enjoying their party foods.

Of all the pleasant occasions of the school year the Christmas season ranked at or near the top of the list. Before very far into December classes were busy at various art projects, many of them involving red and green materials, adorning not only their artboards but overflowing to windows, doors, and hallways throughout the school. I remember some beautiful stained glass windows created by the pupils and taped to their classroom windows. With the sun shining on them they were quite striking.

Some years where classroom space permitted it a Christmas tree was set up in the room. Of course it was adorned with decorations made by the class. Another interesting art project they enjoyed was cutting out snowflakes and suspending them as mobiles from the room's light fixtures. They looked very realistic fluttering around whenever the door was opened. At normal school we learned how to fold a piece of paper in such a way that you could cut out a perfectly hexagonal snowflake.

Christmas music was always a highlight of this festive season. As well as learning new Christmas songs every year we would combine some of the senior classes in the school and sing the old carol favourites as well as Rudolph and Frosty, accompanied by a piano. Sometimes an evening program was put on by the pupils at a Home and School meeting. I remember on one of these joyous evenings we had eight boys wearing cardboard antlers and harnessed together with ropes pulling Santa Claus, complete with a pack of toys, across the stage. All the while they sang Here Comes Santa Claus, who was sitting in a wagon with cardboard sides painted up to look like a sleigh. On the same program one of my brighter pupils recited 'Twas the Night Before Christmas from memory. This was quite an achievement considering the length of that poem.

Some years, when the class was agreeable to it, the pupils drew names and bought gifts, at a nominal cost, to exchange with one another. This practice was suddenly terminated in the late1950s on an order from the director of education. He stated that there would be no more buying and exchanging gifts throughout the public school system.

Now what could be the reason for such a seemingly hard-hearted decision? Apparently the director received word that a teacher in the system not only told her class what gifts she would like from them but even informed them of the colours and sizes of the presents she wished to receive. Can you imagine that? The nerve of some people!

When I told the class about the ban on gift giving some of my grade 8 girls were very upset as they had been doing this for years on their way up through the grades. So on their own volition they confronted the principal with their opposition to this move in the hopes that something could be done about it. After some deliberation he informed them that if they quietly brought their gifts to school and then exchanged them outside the school door on their way home, that would still be in keeping with the letter of the law. This satisfied the girls concerned, but that was the last I heard about exchanging gifts in the school system.

On the last school day in December my classes always concluded the day with the usual Christmas party. They had the festivities of Christmas to look forward to with family and relatives within the next four days, they awaited anxiously for the two weeks of holidays about to begin, and they anticipated the outdoor winter activities that lay ahead such as skating, skiing, and tobogganing. It was indeed a most delightful time of their year.

The valentines day party was more subdued than the other two. Of course we had art lessons where we made valentine cards, cherubs, and hearts with which to decorate the room in the predominant red, pink, and white. The big attraction however was the large cardboard box, suitably adorned, to hold the many valentines the pupils bought into the classroom during the week preceding the party. During that event three of four "mailmen" were selected to deliver the valentines while the class enjoyed their food and beverages. A good time was had by all.

I hope that this chapter has bought back to you some

happy memories both of school party times and the events leading up to them.

MUSIC SUPERVISORS

From a selfish point of view I was always pleased to see the local music supervisor come to my room and take over the class for a half hour or so. Until the teaching of French was introduced into the system in the mid 1960s it was almost the only time when I got a break from being in charge of the class, and it gave me a wonderful opportunity from the back of the classroom to watch my charges in action. Being in a non-participatory role I had a better chance to learn much about them – things such as how clearly they spoke in answering questions, the length of their attention spans, their ability or lack thereof to disregard extraneous sounds beyond the classroom, the degree to which they participated in the music lesson, whether they were fidgeters or sat relatively still, and the like. When the music teacher left I usually returned to the front of the room refreshed and eager to continue with my usual role in the classroom.

I had two rather amusing situations with music supervisors, one very early in my career and the other about twelve years later. One morning when I was in the second week of my teaching profession I heard a knock at the door. I walked to the back of the room, opened the door, and there stood a middle-aged, well-dressed man with a fedora in one hand and a satchel in the other. He tipped his head forward a little as he said good morning and immediately side-stepped me and walked towards the front of the room. I didn't even have a chance to cut him off at the pass. I was flabbergasted.

My first reaction took me back to something they told us during our year of teacher training just a few months earlier.

"Beware of book salesmen trying to peddle their wares while you are teaching." And then, the nerve of this character, he walked right over to my desk and sat down in my chair! There's nothing quite like making yourself at home. While I was pondering about whatever possessed a person to exhibit such strange behaviour, and, what was I to do about this weird situation, I saw the first glimmer of light at the end of the tunnel. All the while the children did not seem perturbed or alarmed at this man's sudden presence in the room. In fact when he sat down they smiled at him. So obviously they knew who he was. When he asked them if they were ready for another year of singing it finally dawned on me. This was not a book salesman but the school's music supervisor. I slumped down, much relieved, into a chair at the back of the classroom.

Obviously there was a decided lack of communication in this whole affair. I was not told that there was a music supervisor who came to the school on a regular basis one day each week, nor was I informed as to what day that was or when during the day he would be in my room. Also it was most unusual, I thought, that he did not at least introduce himself when I first met him at the classroom door. A simple, "Hello, I'm Mr. Revoy, your music supervisor," would have started off our acquaintance much better. Despite his eccentric first entrance into my classroom, Mr. Revoy and I got along very well. He had quite a sense of humour also. Sometimes when he stood up to leave at the end of a visit he would pick up his hat and say to the pupils, "Do you know what my hat is saying to me?" They would immediately reply in unison, "I'm going on a-head." I enjoyed his visits.

The other humourous incident I had with a music supervisor involved Miss Coons, who visited all elementary schools in the city of Peterborough to assist teachers in musical matters. Now Miss Coons has been at this business for quite some time. I well remember when she first became the music supervisor, back in 1939 when I was in grade 4. Our amusing drama took place in 1961.

Miss Coons became a very well-known personality to the thousands of school children she taught over the years. When talking with some of these people I find they remember her especially for three reasons. Whenever a class started to sing, right away she would walk up and down the aisles, her head well bent down so that her ear was almost in the pupils' mouths in order to hear them better, and all that time she tapped out the beat on the pupils' desks with a short baton that was always in her hand. Another thing that stands out in their memories is how she could lead a class in singing up and down the modulator. Many of you will remember I'm sure that chart that hung at the front of the classroom and the numerous times you sang up and down the tonic sol-fa scale: doh, ra, me, fah, soh, lah, te, doh'. Miss Coons had many exercises and drills using those eight notes. The other notable characteristic she had was that she was a prolific talker.

One year when Miss Coons was nearing retirement my principal asked me to help four teachers of senior grades with their music program. I was to visit their classrooms one afternoon a week while a supply teacher taught my class. (Back then there was money to burn in the education business.) My job was to teach new songs one week, the home room teacher would work on them during that week, and I would "polish them up", if necessary, on my next visit. In the spring of that year Miss Coons informed me that she would like to sit in on one of these classes. I was not sure what part she wanted to play that afternoon, but I soon found out. As the two of us entered the classroom she said to the pupils, "Things will be a bit different this time. I'm going to sit down at the back of the room and enjoy your concert led by Mr. Paterson."

That being my cue I had the class sing a couple of songs and after each one Miss Coons commented on the songs and how well she liked the pupils' singing. By the third song I noticed her getting a little restless, and as I might have guessed, she got up while they were singing and began her "bend over and listen to them sing" routine. I knew right then and there that the two of us were in for a short minuet, with her stepping slowly to the front of the room while I gradually retreated to the back. By the time the last verse was finished she was standing proudly facing the class while I sat down in what was still a warm chair.

The poor old soul – like the proverbial punch-drunk boxer who starts swinging whenever he hears a bell ring, Miss Coons couldn't resist the urge to take over a class when she heard one singing. I could not fault her for that; after all, she had spent over half her teaching career conducting classes in the art of singing. The amusing part of it all was that I was the one who sat down at the back of the room and enjoyed the concert. Charlie Benson, the home room teacher, saw this change of command happening as a neutral observer, and found the whole thing to be highly entertaining. In fact, he told me later he had a tough time trying to keep from chuckling while it took place.

NOW HEAR THIS!

What a boon public speaking systems were when they were installed in schools in the 1950s. That's when they appeared on the scene in Peterborough, at least. A PA system is a marvellous device whereby a school principal can send out a message to his staff, the students or pupils, a selected group of classrooms, or everyone in the school, and it's all done by activating switches right in his office.

One wonders how these messages were delivered to their intended receivers before this wonderful device came along. I can well remember as an elementary school pupil seeing our principal pop his head quickly through the classroom door, make an announcement, and depart to the next classroom almost before he finished talking. Since he had only nine other classrooms to visit it didn't take him very long, but it must have been quite a time-consuming chore in larger schools.

We had no PA system when I attended secondary school in the 1940s. To get information to the student body we had daily assemblies in the school auditorium where the principal, staff members, and selected students went up on stage to make their announcements.

In the first three schools where I taught, up to 1958, principals were still delivering messages on foot, but one of them had a time-saving innovation. From his own class he selected a bright pupil for every class in the school. If his message was a simple one he had these runners relay it to their respective teachers, who, if the communication applied to the pupils, in turn relayed it to them.

By the 1960s PA systems were part and parcel in every school and by and large they were used wisely. By that term I mean that most principals used them for their intended purpose, namely to get a message out to people where immediate action or feedback was necessary. By using the PA system only for important communications it meant fewer interruptions in the learning process going on in every classroom.

I well remember one principal who made very few announcements over the PA system. Those he did were always crisp, concise, and right to the point. He preferred to send around written notices appended to a clipboard, so, as he once told me, they wouldn't get lost or buried under other papers often located on teachers' desks.

Once he did use the intercom for what might seem like a trivial reason. At five minutes before dismissal time one spring afternoon the whole school was treated to a grade 6 class singing a lovely, lilting tune entitled Cornish May Song, and they sang it beautifully. Now how did this come about? I'm sure it wasn't pre-planned. What I think happened was when he contacted the grade 6 teacher a minute or two earlier he interrupted their song, and when he finished his business with him he asked that teacher to start the song again. That's when he turned on the all-call switch and we heard this lovely rendition. Everyone enjoyed it, and it was a delightful way to end a school day.

Unfortunately, the "blower" as it was sometimes called was over-used occasionally. For a short duration there was a football league among a limited number of schools in our system. In another school our principal, while not athletic himself, was quite a sports fan. He attended all the games his school played, and sometimes he would give us a blow by blow account next day of a certain game via the PA system. This was not directed just to the senior grades, some of whom would be interested in it, but was broadcast to the entire school population. Whenever he started his football review I tried not to look angry or bored, but it was difficult not to do so. It was an interruption some teachers felt was quite unnecessary.

The kindergarten teacher in that school once told some of us in the staff room one recess just what effect this man's voice had on her pupils when he spoke over the intercom. On these occasions he lowered his voice and spoke slowly, and as a result it sounded quite sepulchral. One time after he had finished his announcement a little fellow asked his teacher, "Is that God speaking?"

While the overuse of the intercom by the principal could be annoying to teachers, in some cases just the opposite occurred. A particular teacher could contact the principal too often about picayune matters to the point that she would get on his nerves. One day a principal, trying to do three or four things at once in his office, heard that teacher's buzzer sound and automatically activated the switch to her room, or so he meant to do. The switch he threw instead was the one he used when he wanted to talk to the whole school. That's when he instinctively uttered his thoughts aloud, "What does that woman want now!" Two things

I wonder about. Did the lady teacher concerned learn anything from this experience, and what did the rest of the school think the principal was talking about?

The Greeks had a good motto when in comes to dealing with things like PA systems – nothing in excess.

STUDENT TEACHERS

When I look back on my earlier years it is no wonder that I became an elementary school teacher. For almost all of those years I lived within a five minute walk to the Peterborough Normal School (later known as a teachers' college) and one of my earliest pre-kindergarten memories was playing on the front steps of that building. The elementary school I attended from kindergarten to grade 8 was Queen Alexandra Public School, which was also only five minutes away from the normal school. Because of its proximity we had normal school students teaching us what were known as unit lessons. These were single lessons about a half hour long, so that the students could get practical experience in regular classroom situations.

Many students from out of town boarded in my neighbourhood and I got to know a few of them on a first name basis every year as I met them on the street quite often. The area around the normal school was almost like an educational village of its own. So throughout much of my life I have had an association with student teachers, first as an elementary school pupil, then as a normal student, and finally as a practice teacher, one who received students in the classroom on their way to becoming teachers.

The unit lessons operated in this fashion from at least the mid-1930s till 1973 when the teachers' college closed. From late

September till May a group of six student teachers would visit on a Thursday afternoon the class they were to teach the following week, and hopefully learn on that occasion some of the tricks of the teaching trade: assemblies and dismissals, classroom routines, storage of materials, the teacher's handling of any problems that arose, etc.

The following week three students taught on Tuesday and the other three on Wednesday. Immediately following the afternoon dismissal the practice teacher would discuss with the three students the strengths and weaknesses of their lessons and offer suggestions for improvement where necessary. Every week the members in each group of six students changed. This was arranged so that over the year each student would witness a greater variety of neophytes in action, and thus learn from their strong and weak points.

My memories of student teachers abound. Here are a few of them that I find very easy to remember. Every now and then the masters at the normal school would ask that a group of about ten pupils from Queen Alexandra be sent over to them, usually in early autumn, so that they could teach this miniature class a typical lesson while a class of students behind them were busy writing down notes. Just before the selected group set out on their educational expedition large name cards were appended to their wearing apparel. I always felt very pleased to be included in one of these groups and enjoyed the experience immensely. A few years later as a student teacher I witnessed this scene again, only this time I was one of those seated behind these groups of pre-teenagers, busily taking notes.

When I was in grade 7 a young lady taught us a lesson about that famous Swiss archer, William Tell. Near the end of the lesson our classroom teacher was momentarily called out of the room. At this point the student teacher, near the end of her dissertation, picked up a bow and arrow she had with her at the front of the room, and proceeded to show us how William Tell would have aimed it. It just so happened that the arrow was aimed at the classroom door, and at that moment in walked our teacher. Being a World War I veteran and a man with a ready sense of humour he immediately threw up both his arms in an act of surrender. Everyone in the room howled with laughter.

The year I was at normal school the science master had an extracurricular club of a few students. He arranged an assembly for the entire student body one May afternoon where each member of his club spoke for a short time about a particular plant or animal. In the normal school there was at that time an eye-catching display of stuffed birds in large glass cases. One girl began her talk about one of these birds while she held it in one hand. Before very long she became rather nervous and her bird-in-the-hand began to shake around. The science master, wishing to help her, interrupted and said, "If you're not careful, Miss Smith, that bird is going to fly right out of your hand." After some laughter from the assembly he continued, "Now just relax for a minute, take a few deep breaths, and then carry on."

Well, his advice worked. She gained her composure and made a good ending to her presentation. That afternoon the science master gave all of us a sample of what is known in teaching as incidental learning. Throughout my career I used his counsel when I too was in a situation where I felt nervous.

One October afternoon three of us taught our weekly unit lessons over at Queen Alex in the grade 1 class. Peter was the first, and he presented a short thanksgiving hymn to the class. This was known as a rote song, whereby the teacher sings the song line by line and the pupils echo each line back to him. Eventually the whole song is put together as a unit. The only problem was that Peter was what was known in the teaching business as an OT (out of tune). In other words he couldn't carry a tune in a basket. He had the first line right but after that his pitch varied all over the place, sometimes too high, sometimes too low, and at rare moments right on.

Most of the little people in front of him took this lesson in their stride, either not knowing he was singing incorrectly or being too polite to make a scene about it. From my position at the back of the room, however, I noticed two little fellows smirking at each other and almost giggling every time Peter sang. They obviously knew he wasn't singing it right. Finally the practice teacher (who, incidentally, had taught me in grade 1) got up from her chair in a back corner of the room, went forward to these two scalawags, and bent down to whisper something into their ears. It was apparent that she admonished them for their misbehaviour as they immediately straightened up. I must admit that until this happened I too was having a very difficult time trying to keep a straight face. I should have felt sorry for Peter's plight but if the truth were known I don't think he realized that anything was amiss. Somehow Peter and the class got through that lesson.

Later that day I thought to myself why didn't each practice teacher receive in mid-September a list of these out of tune students before unit lessons even began? Then every one of them would have been spared Peter's fate.

When I first started to teach in the city I was flattered when they asked me to be a practice teacher. I found that it helped to keep me more attentive in my teaching, especially in the matter of timing. If the students' lessons didn't begin and end on time one of them could end up being short-changed.

In this school I had a problem in this regard. The school bell did not ring automatically, and thus the principal had one of his grade 8 boys, who was not too swift, do the job for him. As a result it was quite common for the afternoon assembly to begin five minutes late, so on the days I had student teachers I would go to the office just before bell time and ring it myself if the official ringer didn't show up on time. Since I was the only teacher in that school who had normal students it became a bit of a joke when the other staff members saw me going to the office to ring the bell.

During the years that I had student teachers most of my classes reacted to them quite well, but occasionally I had a class with a few unruly pupils who would try to rock the boat when we were part way through a monotonous lesson presentation. They started to act as though I was no longer in the room. I soon rectified that, however. I would clear my throat with a quick but loud "Ahem" and immediately the restless waves of disturbance subsided and the ship of education would once again find itself on still waters.

Student teachers – It was great to interact with them as an elementary school pupil, great to be one while learning how to become a teacher, and great to have them in my classroom as a practice teacher with their young outlook on life.

A FAINT SPELL

Have you ever been with a number of people when something happens that triggers the release of an emotion within that group? You can almost feel the "electricity" in the air when an aura descends like an invisible rain and permeates everyone there. Then an innate feeling of sorrow, fear, queasiness, joy, humour, etc, seems to spread from person to person like wildfire. Call it a spell, hex, emanation, whatever, one of my classes experienced this phenomenon during my early years of teaching.

The occasion was the arrival at the school of a local doctor, who was also the medical officer of health for the region, his nurse, and their equipment. They had come to inoculate all the pupils in the school to immunize them against our microbial enemies that try to harm us with winter ailments. Getting the needle was an annual ritual in the village every autumn.

It reminded me of the days when I attended school, and

we received needles once a year when we were in the primary grades. I'll swear those needles were longer and thicker than they are nowadays and were somewhat akin to the giant needles that dentists used to use to freeze a part of your mouth. We received this shot in what was the nurse's room in my elementary school, which is now a community centre. To this day every time I walk by the door of that room I cringe as I recall those unpleasant memories.

Today things are much better. Not only does the needle slip into your arm more smoothly and less painfully but the people administering it have a much more pleasant "bedside manner" than that of the gruff, stern doctors of my childhood. Since the grade 6-7 class I had the year of this impending mishap was quite a normal one and without any over-emotional types I did not anticipate any problems. Yet from my earlier experiences with needles I could readily sympathize with children about to receive one. It isn't a favourite pastime in one's youth.

When it came time for my class to be inoculated we lined up outside the needling room with one shirtsleeve rolled up. I received my shot first to show them how easy and painless it was. After each pupil received his shot he went back to the classroom on his own. All went well, and we were about half way through being immunized when it was Susan's turn to get her needle. Immediately after receiving it she fainted. Of course the doctor and nurse at once looked after Susan's needs before resuming their work and had her rest on a couch nearby while they carried on with their appointed task.

When I got back to the classroom all was not well. Perhaps that should be reworded – all were not well. Some were wiping off their brows with the backs of their sleeves, others were resting their heads face down on their arms upon their desks, and they had rather woebegone looks on their faces. When I asked them what was wrong the general answer I received was that they felt sick. I knew that they were not physically ill, and that this was all "in their heads". Obviously what had happened was that some pupils had seen Susan faint, and on returning to their room immediately spread the news. The result was this scene of mutual commiseration. No doubt some of them thought that they too were going to pass out at any moment, just as Susan did.

I realized as long as they felt this way that they were in no condition to carry on with their regular work of the day. When I looked out the window and saw that it was still a sunny, warm morning I thought of an idea to break this psychological spell – get them outside and moving around. So I announced that we were going outdoors to see if a little fresh air would make us feel better.

Along one edge of the schoolyard was a long line of maple trees. They were quite large, evenly spaced out, and were probably planted there in the late 1800's. We walked down the entire length of this line, zig-zagging back and forth around each tree in turn. It was an invigorating walk under a lovely canopy of red and gold leaves. While we chatted about everything and anything I listened carefully but heard not a word about Susan's fainting.

When we got back to the classroom and sat down I observed that our outdoor walk had done the trick. The pall of fear had lifted, the children had happy looks on their faces again, and all was back to normal. We went back to work at what we were doing before the doctor's visit while Susan rested on the couch until noon, by which time she had fully recuperated and was quite able to walk home accompanied by her best friend. I wondered at the time if Susan were truly aware of the plight her fainting had caused her classmates.

CURRICULUM, CURRICULA

This past summer while looking at some of the work my twin granddaughters did in grade 4 I noticed that they had learned about the different kinds of rocks. This is something I learned in grade 9. There is no doubt that the curriculum has been downgraded, but I feel that children nowadays can handle this. I'll be the first to admit that today's children in the primary grades get off to a better start than my generation did. This is because at an early age they are exposed to educational television, devices that help them learn how to read, and educational games.

When I started teaching the elementary school curriculum consisted of two small books. From at least the 1940s to well on in the 1960s we had the grey course of studies for grades 1 to 6 and the blue one for grades 7 and 8. These books outlined the subject matter to be taught grade by grade in all subjects. They were, shall we say, the teachers' bibles. If a child moved during the school year across a city or across the province the new teacher had a good idea of where his/her new charge should be in subject matter that was sequential.

Just as children grow slowly year by year so too a curriculum changes gradually with the passing of time, due partly to the addition of content, e.g., Science, and to certain changes in our way of living e.g., Health. The Hall-Dennis report, entitled Living and Learning, came on the scene in 1967 and attempted to change things radically, however. The following quotations are taken from that document:

- There is a need for a fresh look at education.

- eliminate lock-step systems of organizing pupils such as grades, streams, and programs

- ensure continuous progress

- abandon the use of percentage marks and letter grades; instead use parent and pupil counselling

- avoid stultifying uniformity

- use computer facilities which will individualize pupil-teacher scheduling

This might be summed up by saying that every pupil should advance through the curriculum at his/her own rate.

While this was a very noble concept I think it was far too utopian to be put into practice. Such a plan brings some questions to mind. Was the huge cost of audio-visual equipment, especially computers and programing, calculated to carry out this plan? With many different levels of individual progress going on in a classroom how does one teacher measure each child's progress? (I thought it was marvellous that primary teachers could handle three units in one classroom back in the days of the unit system.) Finally, would parents understand such a system where there appears to be no norm, standard, grade, whatever, for the children in a given classroom? How would they know where their child(ren) stood in relation to the expected norm of pupils of a given age? I don't think John Q. Public would buy such a plan.

Well, forty years later we still have grades and percentage marks or letter ratings on report cards, but not individual progress through the curriculum. Some teachers, however, did accept the innovative tenor of Living and Learning. Two examples I witnessed come to mind from the 1970s, both at the grade 6 level. One teacher was teaching indirect objects of verbs, which at that time was one of the last things in sentence analysis that pupils learned in grade 8. Another teacher taught the products of Romania. (He was of Anglo-Saxon lineage). What was wrong with Canadian products? Sad to say it became an era of teach what you want when you want. At this time many new courses of study appeared. Was the ministry of education trying to get some semblance of unity in the curriculum across the province once again? When excessively radical ideas are introduced into society they are not very likely to succeed e.g., open concept and non-graded schools of the 1960s.

This whole notion that everyone should function at his own rate is not in keeping with either our social or legal conventions. For example, at a large banquet the serving ladies will bring in each successive course of the meal when most people are ready for it. If you wolf down your food in a hurry you will only have to wait awhile for the next course to come along. On the other hand if you dawdle and nibble at your food you may find yourself still eating when the guest speaker starts his spiel. So to some extent you are obliged to eat at a certain rate. Likewise when driving a car on a highway it is dangerous to go too fast or too slowly as both can result in accidents. That's why we have speed limits, so that people should drive with the flow of traffic. Can you picture eight rowers in a race with each one stroking at his own speed? Or workers on an assembly line working ahead of or behind the rate at which the line is moving? Or a choir or an orchestra where one member is out of sync with the others? Much of what we do in life where other people are involved is done at a mutually agreed upon pace. This is true of most occupations. Two exceptions that come to mind are authors and self-employed artists.

I don't see why a group of young people, excepting geniuses and handicapped children, cannot go through their yearly curriculum together. These children, a mini-society, are travelling along the curriculum under the guidance of a teacher who sets the rate of movement along that course. Cannot the whole class learn together, for example, the concept of area? Isn't that more economical of both time and effort? This idea of learning together gives a class a sense of cohesiveness that isn't found when you have a "smart" group, an average group, and a "slow" group learning at different rates. Years ago in music classes in the primary grades they used to brand children as bluebirds, robins, or crows. Don't think for a minute those youngsters didn't know the meaning of the stigma behind those labels. Sure, the bright ones will learn more quickly and the slower ones will need reinforcement when a new lesson is reviewed another day, but isn't that life? So later in the week the teacher gives the class seatwork on area problems, and naturally the smarter pupils will finish ahead of the others. What to do? Make that last problem a real poser to get them digging a little deeper into the subject matter. Also, if these brighter pupils are that clever they should be able to find something worthwhile to do on their own. That was one advantage of the one-room rural schools. When a pupil in that situation finished an assignment he jolly well found something profitable to do or else.

How successful the pupils are in travelling along a curriculum is largely dependent upon the teacher, who feeds them intellectually day after day. If they are fed bite sized pieces, spiced up with proper variety in the menu and served with suitable motivation, they will digest the food for thought that is served to them.

THINGS I REMEMBER

The following is a hodgepodge of anything and everything connected with school.

1. Eagle-eye Taunton

Miss Taunton was definitely a teacher from the old school. Not only was she a stern disciplinarian in her classroom but she ruled with an iron fist while supervising the line of boys coming in from the playground at bell time and ascending the stairs to the second storey of the school. (Oh yes, in those days there were separate entrances for each of the sexes. Things were done properly in those days, you know.) Wintertime was her specialty. From her lofty position at the north end of the hall she had a commanding view of the boots of every boy who entered the building and woe betide any of them that had even the least bit of snow on his boots.

That woman had eagle eyes. I'll swear she could spot a snowflake on a boot fifty feet away from her, and she soon let the miscreant bearer of it feel her wrath. "Get back outside and get that snow off!" she would roar at him. None of the other boys in the line dared to laugh at his fate for fear of receiving a worse reprimand from eagle-eye Taunton. To her fellow staff members she was both a source of amusement and annoyance. Some of them felt that a little bit of snow on a boy's boot wasn't a big deal, and that a little moisture in the dry air of a classroom was actually beneficial.

2. A Bluff beside a Bus

At one school where I taught the distance to any other school with Home Economics and Industrial Arts facilities was so great that my grade 8 class had to travel to one of them by bus rather than walk. The first afternoon in September that they did this presented no problem. The next week, however, there was a difficult situation. Her name was Ruth. Most of the class had boarded the bus when three excited girls came running back into the school to tell me that Ruth refused to get on the bus.

Naturally I went out right away to see what was the matter. Ruth, a nervous person at the best of times, was unusually flustered on this occasion. On asking her why she did not want to get underway with the others she refused to give a direct answer, but merely stated that she did not want to go. There were only two reasons I could imagine why she balked. Either she had had an unpleasant experience with her classmates on the bus the week before or something in the Home Economics class had aroused the memory of some dreadful happening in her earlier childhood.

I did my utmost to calm her down and tried to reason with her but to no avail. By this time the bus should have started on its way, so time was becoming a factor in this dilemma. Moreover, I had no intention of babysitting Ruth for the rest of the afternoon so I made a bold move. I said to her, "Ruth, either you get on this bus now or else I'll pick you up and carry you on." Well, the thought of this happening in front of her peers settled her down somewhat. After a moment's reflection she marched up the steps into the bus and sat down. Mission accomplished. For the rest of the year there was no problem getting her to go to Home Economics class. Whatever her phobia had been she got over it.

It was a good thing for me she got on that bus, as I had no intention of touching her to carry out my bluff. Short of contacting her parents or calling for the assistance of the school board's psychologist I didn't know what else I could have done.

3. An Unexpected Holiday

In the village school where I began my teaching career we had a health problem every year, usually in mid-March. That month heralded the arrival of the sniffles, snort, and sneeze season, when some infectious bug ran rampant throughout the school. Some years, when it was bad enough, the local medical officer of health would close down the school for a couple of days in an attempt to quell this epidemic. You might think that during this unexpected holiday these bouts of coughing would now be prolonged on the streets of the village, at the local arena, etc., but almost anything would be better than allowing this contagion to spread at will in a schoolhouse where upwards of forty children (yes, we had large classes back then in the 1950s) were corralled in the close quarters of a classroom.

There is no doubt that both teachers and pupils enjoyed this unforeseen hiatus. In those days schools did not get a March break in the middle of the month as they do nowadays. Instead we had to wait for the Easter holidays to come along, anywhere from late March to just past mid-April.

In one of those years, about twenty minutes before school was dismissed, the principal called me out to the hall to tell me about this unplanned holiday. Since he was just on his way to make this announcement to every class I wondered why he bothered to tell me privately about it first. I think he felt so good about this sudden time off that he just had to unload on someone. Since I taught across the hall from him I was it.

He broke the news to me in a slow, serious voice, but through it all I knew, especially by the glint in his eyes, that underneath it all he was very happy. I followed his lead and pretended to take this matter seriously, although I too found it difficult to hide my true feelings. He then went on his way to make a quick announcement to every class.

And how did my class react to this news? They had to restrain themselves to keep from cheering.

4. A Slight Oversight

Here's a scene you may have witnessed or even been a part of in your school days. A class is all lined up at the door with the teacher at the head of the line, all waiting for the bell to ring at the end of the school day. The reason for this intended fast getaway is that the teacher probably has some appointment, commitment, tryst, or whatever, and has to get to it as soon as possible after school is over for the day.

In my thirty-five years of teaching I've seen this twice where the pupils were all bundled up in their winter clothing, lunch boxes in one hand or knapsack in place, all set for the bell to ring. The teacher of course was standing in the forefront all set to shoo them away at the first sound of the bell. As long as it's not a daily dismissal routine I suppose these jack-rabbit starts meet the letter of the law.

On one occasion within our school system we had one of these quick takeoffs where everything was not planned out as well as it should have been. There was no doubt that the teacher concerned was giving all his attention to his upcoming business. The proof of that was, when the bell rang he hurried out the classroom door at the back of the room, and, believe it or not, he forgot to dismiss his pupils!

Well, as they sat there they probably thought that he had to see another teacher briefly before he left the school, or that he was attending to some urgent matter concerning a pupil out in the hall. The time must have hung very heavily on their hands while they were waiting for what should have been their teacher's return to the classroom. They would have been sure to hear other pupils in the hall on their way home, free as the proverbial birds, while they were still confined to their room. At last one brave lad proclaimed to the class that he was fed up with waiting and was going home. When he got up out of his chair the others quickly followed his lead.

I don't know if that teacher was censured for his obvious oversight but I do know this matter made some interesting reading in the local newspaper shortly thereafter.

5. A Spelling Slip-up

One evening during parent interviews I had a unique experience during an interview with one mother. (Yes, before professional activity days came along twenty years later parent interviews were held in the evening hours, not in school time.) This set of interviews came, as usual, soon after report cards had been sent home to show the progress pupils had made during the previous term. Things were going quite well I thought, with this mother of a boy who was an average pupil academically in his grade 7 year. Near the end of this session, however, she became slightly belligerent over the fact that I had not given son Rob a higher mark in spelling. In other classrooms he had always received quite high marks, she said, and according to her son he had usually done very well on his weekly spelling dictations. With this I readily agreed, but I knew something about the spelling in Rob's day to day work that she was not aware of.

Rather than just telling her that Rob's spelling in his other written work was slightly atrocious I figured it would be better to show her this. So I took Rob's workbook from his desk, opened it at random, picked up a red pen and began indicating spelling errors while she looked on. I forget how many mistakes I found but when I was finished it looked as though those two pages had the measles. The look on her face suggested that she got the message all right. When the bell rang shortly thereafter to signal the end of that interview I'm sure this lady must have walked through the door, figuratively speaking, with her tail between her legs.

Perhaps ultimately her misunderstanding had been my fault. Maybe I should have informed parents, and especially my pupils, that the spelling mark they received on their report cards wasn't based solely on the result of their spelling dictations, but also on their accuracy in that subject in all written work I checked, such as notebooks, compositions, book reports, and the like.

It's one thing to do well at something when you're in the limelight with it, but it's another thing when you do poorly at it in your run-of-the-mill daily work. This is one of the weaknesses in our human nature and I suppose we are all guilty of it at times.

6. Let's Be Clear about This

You may recall from your school days that your teachers asked you to write expository paragraphs. Rather than telling a story or describing something, this type of paragraph explains how to do something, or how a thing works. It also includes giving your opinion about a particular matter. Unless the writer expresses himself clearly, orderly, and completely, it is sometimes difficult to get the drift of what he is trying to communicate. (Have you ever had trouble trying to follow the directions about how to put together a child's unassembled Christmas gift?) Sometimes writing an expository paragraph can be more difficult than you think.

To show classes how brain racking this can be I gave them this assignment. Tell me how to do up a button. When they were finished that's when the fun began. I said that I would stand up at the front of the room, and as volunteers read their paragraphs I would follow their instructions and go through the motions of doing up my suitcoat button just as they had told me to do.

Every year most pupils would say something like this. "Grab the button in one hand and the button hole in the other and push the button through the hole." I of course grabbed the button and buttonhole in each fist and said those directions wouldn't work. At this stage other volunteers would respond with an improved version that read roughly, "Take hold of the button with the fingers and thumb on your right hand and the buttonhole with the left hand fingers and thumb. Bring the two together and push the button through the hole." With these directions I could bring the button beside the buttonhole now but they still didn't tell me how to move that button through the hole.

By now the list of volunteers had shrunk considerably. Many pupils realized then and there that their paragraphs were just not explicit enough to do the job. So at this juncture I would ask, "Do any of you think you can tell me how to do up this button?" Generally two or three thought they could. We listened to all of their paragraphs and then decided who had done the best job of it.

The winner's explanation was close to this. "Take hold of the button on its outward edge with the right thumb and index finger, and hold the cloth on the inside edge of the buttonhole with the left thumb and index finger. Now bring your two hands together. As you push the button through the buttonhole grab it with your left thumb and index finger. Transfer your right thumb to the edge of the button. With the ends of your left fingers pull the button the rest of the way through the hole."

If you think that was a tough nut to crack try this one in your spare time – how to tie up a shoelace.

7. A Dirty Trick

At one school we had a caretaker who had this thing about mud. He hated it. I can't say I blamed him, when you consider it was his job to sweep it up off the floors at the end of the school day and get rid of it, so the less of it there was in the school the easier his job would be. He tried to accomplish this in two ways. First of all on those muddy April mornings he would position himself in front of the pupils' entrance to the school, and as the line proceeded into the building he inspected the footwear of every pupil.

From my vantage point on the second storey hallway I sometimes looked down on the slow moving line of children below, and watched the mud inspection take place. Joe, the caretaker, rarely stopped talking. He reprimanded them continually, and his favourite blast, "Get that mud off your boots!" could be heard upstairs through closed windows. Those with muddy boots took him at his word as they stepped out of line and endeavoured to scrape their footwear clean. No doubt this early morning castigation saved him a lot of late afternoon elbow grease.

But a few of those with muddy footwear occasionally slipped into school past his careful gaze, and at the end of the day there would be a noticeable amount of dust (dried up mud) under the desks of these individuals. That's when he put his second plan of attack into action. When he came to a desk with this situation he swept the pile of dust into his dustpan, and then, believe it or not, he threw it into the pupil's desk on top of his books! Had I not witnessed this scene while working at my desk after school one day I would never have believed such a thing could happen.

This wasn't the only time Joe played this dirty trick on a mud-laden pupil. I found out that it happened in other classrooms as well. The interesting thing is as far as I know he never received any censure for committing this act. The guilty boys probably didn't tell their teachers or parents about it for fear that they would receive further reproof for bringing mud into the school. I'm sure they knew all too well how the dust got into their desks. There was one beneficial result from all this, however. That muddy-booted pupil of mine never brought another speck of mud into the classroom.

8. I Was Wrong

You aren't very long in the teaching business before you have the pupils in a new class labelled. You think this one will be the brain of the class, that this one is sure to be the class clown, another is the day-dreamy type, while yet another is an attention seeker. And so it goes.

I think teachers are fairly good at this selective process, but every now and then a particular pupil will fool you. Take Dora for instance. Dora was a tall girl who sat in the back left corner of the room, while the windows were on the right side of the classroom. Everything about her seemed to suggest that while her body was in the classroom her mind was obviously somewhere else. There was a glazed look to her eyes, and when she wasn't reading or writing she was looking across the room out the window. When she did look down at her desk it was to watch herself playing with her hands. She was the prime example of a day-dreamer.

As you might expect this personality trait came to my attention early in the school year. When I was teaching a typical lesson where I was questioning the class and developing a blackboard summary as we went along Dora seemed to be out on another planet. So I said to myself I'd better do something to bring her back down to earth.

One time I asked a question while looking out the window, paused for a moment, and then called on Dora for an answer. I was surprised that she gave a good answer right away. Thinking that this was just a lucky fluke, another time I asked a question while looking straight down at the pupil in front of my desk, and immediately fired out Dora's name. Again she gave back a correct answer without hesitation. By now I was beginning to think differently about her day-dreaming. Here was a girl who seemingly was away out in left field all the time but obviously could pay attention to what was going on in the classroom while gazing outside the window.

I was no longer worried about her being left out of the picture. If she could apparently day-dream yet be right on top of the work at hand, then more power to her. She was one of my top pupils in that class, and almost fifty years later a fellow classmate of hers told me that she became a successful high school teacher.

Sometimes they fool you.

9. A One-way Attraction

I found out early in my teaching career that some grade 8 girls have their eyes set on young, single, and unattached male teachers. While walking on my way home from school I remember on different occasions some of them calling out to me, "Hellooooo Mr. Patersonnnnnnn." Not wanting to get their hopes up or start an undesired relationship I would answer back in an expressionless voice the simple answer, "Hello," hoping that this would cool their ardour. Considering the difference between their age and mine I suppose these "love calls" were natural enough. After all I was only six years older than they were.

Interestingly enough, when they discovered that I had found myself a female companion of my vintage they completely ignored me. Needless to say I wasn't broken-hearted, and I hoped they weren't either.

Later in my teaching years I witnessed this same phenomenon occurring with two young male teachers with the same end result. Oh well, hope springs eternal in the human breast.

10. A Real Joker

At one school we had a principal who just couldn't wait to tell everyone he came in contact with the latest joke he heard. First his secretary heard the joke, then the staff he met throughout the day, and also any visitors who came to his office (and some days they were numerous). Since his office and my classroom backed on to one another I could at times hear him laughing, and I assumed after awhile that he was chuckling over another one of his jokes he had told during a telephone conversation.

For those of us close to his office these jokes became a source of annoyance after hearing the same one being told over and over for a few days. At the end of one school day I was walking past the secretary's room just as she was putting on her coat to leave. From the principal's inner office we suddenly heard a loud guffaw. She looked at me disgustedly and said, "If I hear that joke once more I'll scream!"

11. Angel or Devil ?

In my very first month of teaching I had a trying experience dealing with two people. One was Arnold, a pupil in my class, and the other was his mother, Mrs. Fee. Now Arnold was the kind of pupil who came to my attention on day one. He was self-centred, attention-seeking, outspoken, and he disturbed the pupils who sat near him. I was obliged to reprimand him on several occasions that first week of school. If I didn't do it at the start I felt it would be like letting a small fire become a blazing inferno in a few weeks' time. In short, Arnold was not the kind of pupil you would want to have in your first class.

The second problem arose when Mrs. Fee began her periodic phone calls. She claimed that I was "picking on" her son. Of course I was but I didn't tell her that. (Obviously Arnold did not like being put in his place, and had gone to mother for support.) When I explained to her Arnold's problems mentioned above I'm sure she did not believe me. She insisted that he was a very well behaved boy at home, and I in turn found that hard to believe. While he may have been an angel at home I knew he was a little devil at school.

Her phone calls followed a definite pattern. She would call about fifteen minutes before the afternoon assembly and keep me on the phone trying to convince me that I was wrong in my opinion of Arnold, since he was such a nice boy around the house. Finally the bell would ring and thankfully I could tell her I had to leave to teach the class.

In hindsight I can see that I was partly to blame for this situation. I was as green as grass at the job, and thus had no experience in dealing with a problem child, nor with the vexation of a mother who could not or would not believe that her child was something less than a saint when he wasn't under her wing in the nest.

But fortunately things improved around the end of September. Arnold was starting to fit in to the class situation better, and his mother's phone calls ceased at about this time. Perhaps there were two reasons why the situation improved when it did. Maybe after a month I had learned to rein in Arnold's unruly behaviour and maybe Mrs. Fee reached a point where she realized that perhaps Arnold's demeanour could be less than angelic beyond the home. While he didn't reach sainthood that year we did get along together reasonably well for the rest of the year.

12. Beat the Cash Register

Here's a bit of mental arithmetic that I used to teach that is really very practical every time you buy something at a store. By using it you can tell the clerk what change you should receive before that figure appears on the cash register. Here's how it works. Let's say you bought something worth $3.68 and you gave the clerk a five dollar bill. The transaction would look like this.
$$\begin{array}{r} \$5.00 \\ -3.68 \\ \hline \$1.32 \end{array}$$

You start to calculate your change by working from the left in what I call the dollars column, then move to the right to the dimes column, and finally over to the cents column. In your change the dollar column (1) plus the figure just above it (3) will add up to one less than the top figure (5) i.e., 3+1= 4, which is one less then five. Now in the dimes column the lower two numbers will add up to nine, i.e., 3 + 6 = 9. In the cents column the bottom two figures add up to ten, i.e., 2 + 8 = 10. You might like to verify this by adding the bottom two numbers to get the top one.

Now try this one. $20.00 - $8.52 = ? Did you arrive at

$11.48? It's so simple you can do it in five seconds. If there are zeros in the dimes or cents columns this formula may vary somewhat, but it's easy to make the necessary adjustments.

I suggested to my class that they try this method out each time they were going through the check-out line when shopping with their parents. I told them that if you could tell the clerk what change you should get back before it shows up on the cash register, she would think you were one smart kid. Some of them told me they did this, and that the clerks were amazed. Their most common response was, "How did you do that so fast?"

13. A Prolific Talker

I'm not sure where today's teachers are when an assembly bell rings but in my day we stood outside the classroom door or at the top of nearby stairways to supervise incoming pupils. One year a fellow teacher, Terry, and I stood at the upper end of a staircase, one of us on each side, for that purpose. Now children moving through the halls and stairways in lines were to walk in a quiet, orderly fashion, but Terry sure didn't help that cause. With his loud strident voice he could easily be heard quite some distance away, and invariably he would start up a conversation with me as soon as we were stationed in our supervisory positions. I tried not to respond to him as teachers talking while the lines passed by them did not set a good example. That matter didn't bother Terry. When he did stop momentarily in his verbosity he would hear a pupil talking in line and bellow out "No talking in the line there!" A few moments later he took up his conversation with me again. Talk about the pot calling the kettle black! Terry was an excellent example of that old adage, do as I say, not do as I do.

14. A Dangerous Gamble

My grade 8 class at one school had to walk to a neighbouring school to partake of their Home Economics and Industrial Arts classes. This involved crossing a footbridge over the Otonabee River, which bisects the city of Peterborough. One winter day, for some reason yet unknown, Carl did not cross the river by means of the bridge but instead walked across the ice from one bank of the river to the other. One can only surmise why he took this dangerous route. It was likely either to impress the girls or to show his male classmates how brave he was.

Carl probably had no perception of the great danger he was in when he attempted this foolhardy venture. A short distance downstream from the bridge is one of the ten dams that span the Otonabee River, the upper part of which has a very steep gradient. As a result it has a very strong current.

The thickness of the ice above the dam depends mainly on the fluctuation of the temperature. If we have a warm spell the ice in the middle section of the river disappears completely, and then when the weather turns much colder, suddenly the river freezes over entirely once again. Having travelled for many years along a street overlooking this site I have often witnessed this change from ice coverage to open water and back again. Thus it is not safe to try to cross the ice on this river at any time. Carl did not know how lucky he was to still be alive after his derring-do.

A girl in our classroom told me a couple days later about Carl's escapade, but I did not chastise him for his foolish behaviour. It was after the fact anyway, and I was thankful that he came out of it alive. I did have a brief conversation with him after school, however, and explained how the thickness of the ice can vary greatly in a few days depending on the weather, and that he was fortunate to still be alive. I concluded by telling him he was lucky his classmates didn't have to attend his funeral. End of sermon.

15. What's Your Viewpoint?

Have you ever thought about this one? If, as a pupil or a teacher, you could have your choice as to which direction your classroom windows faced, what would your choice be – north, south, east or west? Let's go around the compass and see what advantages or drawbacks each direction offers.

Early in my career I taught in two classrooms where the windows faced north. About the only good thing I can say for this setup is that you don't have to worry about being blinded by the sun. On the negative side the constant lack of direct sunlight all year can be depressing. Also, other things being equal, cold winds from the north can penetrate poorly fitting windows more easily on that side of the school.

Now we take a quarter turn to the western viewpoint, where the advantage is that you are facing neither cold arctic blasts or heat waves from southern climes. In the fall and winter it's pleasant to have the afternoon sunlight, but in June that can be another story. In two of the three classrooms where I faced westward there was a paved area just below the windows. Towards the latter part of the school year the temperature in our classroom was almost unbearable during a heat wave.

With a southern exposure you're on the sunny side of the school. In winter that sunlight is most welcome, but I can remember some hot Septembers, Mays, and Junes when we didn't have much relief from a fiery sun heating up the south side of the building all day.

That leaves us with an eastern perspective. In my estimation this is the preferred side of a school building. Like the west side of the school you get a fair share of direct sunlight during the school hours of the day, but unlike the west side the sun shining through east facing windows in the morning isn't overpowering the way it is when it glares through the glass on the west side of a building in the afternoon. Moreover, I found that the morning sun beaming in on us at the start of the school day acted as a pleasant wake up call to prepare us for this business of learning. I can find no drawbacks to having windows facing to the east, and in three schools I was happy with this situation. That's my viewpoint anyway.

16. A Strange Request

When I moved to another school one year I met up with an unusual experience not very long after school started in September. A teacher in the primary grades was on yard duty one morning. Shortly before 9:00 A.M. she arrived at my door with three woebegone ragamuffins in tow, and calmly said to me, in my role as vice principal, "Mr. Paterson, I want you to strap these boys for misbehaviour." That was the sum total of all she said. I waited for her to give me some reason why these three should be punished, but I didn't get one. As a matter of fact she had no time for one as she simply turned on the spot and walked away! She had done her duty; now the rest was up to me. What strange conduct this was on her part, I thought.

I looked at them sagaciously and asked them what they had done to deserve punishment. Their answers were quite vague. Further questioning revealed that they were in Grade 3. I thought to myself boys that young are not likely to cause any serious trouble so early in the day. Instead of strapping them (I had no valid reason to do so), I took their names and told them not to come to this teacher's attention from now on, and that if they were brought to me again I might not let them off so easily next time. Thus ended an unusual beginning of a school day.

17. If He Passes / If She Fails

Sometimes parents try in strange ways to motivate teachers or pupils to ensure that their children will pass on to the next grade. At the end of an interview with the father of a boy in my classroom he informed me that if his son Jack passed in June he would buy him a bicycle. Now wasn't that putting me on the spot? I didn't comment on his statement, but instead I smiled at him in such a way as to give him this message: I know your game, I'll do what is best for your son, and let's hope that things work out all right. Incidentally, he passed.

The other case was a sad one. Back in the 1950's neither

parents nor pupils were informed as to whether a child passed or not before the last afternoon of school in June. One year after I gave out the final report cards, the bell rang, the class was dismissed, and I busied myself clearing up odds and ends at my desk. I happened to look up and saw a girl seated with her head on her arm, sobbing. I immediately went back to offer assistance. She told me that her dad had said if she did not pass she could not go swimming at the local beach all summer. The poor girl had to repeat her year, and now she was afraid to go home and give him this news.

I had met the father a few times, and he did not seem like a person who would put a child in a situation like this. Such motivation! Had he given any thought to the consequences if his scheme failed?

So I offered to drive the girl home and have a talk with her father. When he opened the door after my knock I knew I had caught him by surprise. Here I was with her report card in my hand and his dejected-looking daughter beside me. When I told him what his daughter had said to me he hemmed and hawed a bit and then said, "Oh sure, she can go swimming all right." He knew right then and there that he had been too demanding of his child, which only goes to show that sometimes people say things they don't really mean to.

18.Screeeech!

Throughout my teaching career I did not consider maintaining classroom discipline to be a major problem. As I look back over those years I think by and large my pupils and I got along reasonably well. I don't mean to brag when I say this. Actually it wasn't so much a matter of learning how to discipline classes. Instead I believe it was unknowingly inherited from the many teachers I had, both at elementary and secondary school, who had the knack of keeping law and order. Without that desirable classroom atmosphere learning in school is difficult. When I had teachers, most of them thank goodness, who instilled in us that we were in school to learn, I learned. When I had teachers who did not require us to toe the line I'm sorry to say that I frittered away a lot of time in their classes, and can't remember much of what I learned from them.

Teachers are salespeople, but they don't sell a tangible product. Instead they sell their disciples (learners) things that are of greater worth such as attitudes, skills, work habits, knowledge, and values such as sharing and co-operation. So whatever ability I had for keeping things running smoothly in the classroom I owed it to those "model" teachers whom I was subconsciously emulating.

Every few years, however, I received in September a class containing a few rapscallions who were more bent on mischief than on learning. In any classroom this is most noticeable when the teacher's back is to the class, as is the case when he/she is writing on the blackboard. If a teacher is writing for any length of time there are audible signs that trouble may be brewing – a sudden whisper, the slight movement of a chair, or a dropped ruler.

I think I had a unique cure for this kind of nonsense. I did not turn around quickly and glare at them, but kept on writing, only I held the chalk in a slightly different way. Now I'm sure you know what's coming. Remember when a piece of chalk was drawn across a blackboard the right (wrong?) way? It produced a horrifying sound like the screech of a banshee, and sent a shiver up your spine. As a youngster I remember the same effect when a heavy metal object was dragged across a sidewalk.

That was my way of stopping this misbehaviour. As the chalk scraped along there would be a few sudden gasps followed by absolute silence. I would stop writing momentarily to let the silence penetrate this drama, and then say without turning around, "There now, things sound much better behind me." After I finished writing I turned towards the class and smiled, as much as to say thank you for coming back to order.

I rarely had to do this a second time to a class. They knew right away that if they tried any more of their shenanigans they would get another bout of scraping and screeching.

19. (In)appropriate Music

At one school we had a caretaker named Bert who had a beautiful singing voice, and because he sang so much he was known as the singing caretaker. We never knew when he would start to sing as he made his rounds through the school, but when he did his deep, rich voice penetrated every nook and cranny in the building. Bert was also a talented whistler, and between these two means of communication we soon knew where he was.

Now, much as I enjoy listening to a good singer I believe there is a proper time and place for it, and in my humble opinion the halls of learning when classes are in session are not acceptable venues for it to occur. It seems that in many cases Bert would start up with his powerful voice when I was at a key point in a lesson and throw us all off topic a bit.

I disliked the idea of stopping him from singing while he went about his business but at an opportune time I had a talk with him about this matter. Had he worked in some other locales he could have sung freely all day but I tried to get him to understand that when pupils were at work in a school it was not the proper setting (especially since he had such a booming voice). He was far from happy with my request, but he reluctantly stopped singing and whistling during school hours. We still enjoyed hearing him before school started and after it ended each day.

By an interesting coincidence when I moved to a different school Bert also arrived there two years later. The following incident proves he had no grudge against me about our differences in our former school. One day after school while I was finishing odds and ends at my desk Bert entered the room to sweep up, carrying a mop in one hand and a wastepaper basket in the other. I wondered why he had the latter with him. Suddenly he ceremoniously turned the basket upside down, spilling several papers to the floor.

"What's up, Bert?" I asked in surprise.

"Well," he answered, "If I have to clean your floor I might as well make the job worthwhile."

Talk about an indirect compliment! I chuckled, Bert mopped, and even began singing a bit of a song in his melodious, operatic voice. All's well that ends well.

20. <u>From Phantasy to Reality</u>

One midwinter afternoon I thought I had a professional hockey player in my grade 7 classroom. The background leading up to the scenario went like this. The pupils in that school were very fortunate to have an ice skating rink on their schoolyard thanks to a grade 8 teacher who organized the making of it and his pupils who flooded it and shovelled it off when it was necessary. It provided classes with skating time in their Physical Education periods and was enjoyed by hockey enthusiasts when school was finished for the day.

Most of my pupils were very pleased to have the opportunity to skate in school time. There were, however, a very few of them who did not know how to skate, and the school rule for these pupils was that they were to go to the library for a reading period while the rest of us were outside. They headed to the library at the same time we wended our way to the rink.

On the day in question I noticed that one of my more athletic boys, who had always skated with us before that particular day, was not putting on his winter clothing to join us. When I asked him why he wasn't going outside with us I was utterly amazed by the reply he gave me.

"I have a big hockey game on tonight and I don't want to dull my skates before I play." Can you imagine that! This from a grade 7 boy. Maybe he was fantasizing that he played in the NHL or on one of their farm teams.

I looked at him rather coldly and said. "Go home and get those skates and be back at our rink in fifteen minutes." He did, and he was.

21. Fun Stunts

In teaching Physical Education during my latter years on the job I used to give the class homework in that subject. It was not mandatory and besides I had no way of checking to see that they completed their assignments. In fact it might have been labeled fun homework.

Heaven knows a lot of them needed it. By the 1970s I noticed that by and large many pupils were not in good physical shape. Their legs were all right as most of them could jog around the schoolyard or the G.P. room quite well, but they seemed to have weak arms. Doing even a few pushups was quite a chore for many of them.

Now what was the reason for this lack of strength in their arms? Slowly but surely equipment powered by gasoline and electricity was replacing devices which people once operated by muscle power – snow blowers instead of snow shovels, powered lawn mowers instead of manual push types, outboard motorboats instead of rowboats and canoes, and lately leaf blowers instead of hand rakes. No wonder children were getting out of shape. They were not getting enough exercise.

The work I assigned consisted of physical stunts, and I tried to introduce one each week. They were short, challenging exercises, with most of them needing no equipment. These were done individually and showed how nimble, agile, and spry children were. Here are three typical ones I have selected.

The first one sounds simple enough, but most people have likely never done it. You try to get on your feet from a sitting position without using your hands to get up. The majority of young people can do this one without too much effort.

You may have seen the next one in those old cowboy movies. Jump into the air and try to click your heels together three times before your feet touch the floor. One time is a cinch. Twice takes a bit of effort. Three times is nearly impossible. Try it and you'll find out.

The third stunt takes both skill and courage. Take a lightweight stick e.g., a hockey stick or broomstick, and hold it in front of your body with your hands hip width apart. Then jump up quickly over the stick without letting go of it. You have to be careful in doing this stunt that you don't trip yourself on the stick.

Now for two variations. With the stick held behind your back, jump over it backwards so that it ends up in front of you. Finally, you're a real pro if you can continuously jump forward and backward over the stick three times without pausing.

Here's the homework part of it. I would tell the class to try these stunts at home, and get the family involved in them as well. They are more fun if you make them a family affair.

22. A Religious Parting

I remember being called into the office to be a witness for a strapping about to take place. The principal had four older boys lined up as I entered the room, after which he gave them a very good lecture about the importance of following school rules. Their offence on this occasion was throwing snowballs while on the playground, which was not permitted at that school. After he had strapped them he concluded this incident with a terse biblical quotation. Now I never considered this man to be overly religious, but what he said to them was very apropos. He dismissed them with that well known sentence found in chapter 8 of St. John's gospel, "Go, and sin no more." Despite the solemnity of the occasion I had a hard time to keep from chuckling when he said it.

23. Skip into Spring

One of the surest signs that spring is just around the corner is the sight of girls putting their skipping ropes into action at school. At this time of the year I enjoyed getting outside at recesses to watch them partake of this harbinger of spring. Back in the early 1950s teachers at the village school were not required to be on yard duty four times a day. Besides, everyone on the playground seemed to get along quite well with one another. From an upstairs window overlooking the scene below it was a very rare time that I saw any dissension among the pupils.

But back to skipping. It was quite a delight to see the various groups of girls, each with their own section of sidewalk, jumping up and down at different rates, some fast, some slow. The part of it I liked best, however, was walking from one group to another and listening to the variety of lilting tunes and singsong chants they uttered, always with a strong beat in order to help them jump in time and not get tangled up in a rope. As I moved during my career I noticed these skipping songs differed from school to school. Just think of the hundreds of them there must be from across the breadth of this country. If someone hasn't already compiled a book of them they should. To me that would be a real piece of Canadiana.

24. An Unusual Gift

When I moved to a brand new school one September the staff therein were the recipients of an interesting gift. The school was in the suburbs of the city, and like many communities during the years of the baby boom new schools were needed to accommodate the families in the numerous houses built on the periphery of cities, towns, and villages across the country. One of the eight classrooms in this building, however, was not yet required to receive a class of pupils in its first years, so the powers that be in the local board of education put this room to another use. It was to become the board room for the Peterborough public school system.

Apparently a larger room was needed to provide for the commodious table and several chairs used by the school board and upper level administrators when they sat down to make their educational deliberations. And what grand furniture it was! The beautiful wooden table with its smooth, polished top took up a considerable area of that classroom. Around it were, as I recall, about sixteen large, comfortable armchairs the backs and seats of which were covered with rich, crimson-coloured leather.

The school staff considered this board room, which was used for its intended purpose only in the evenings, as a gift. Whenever we had staff meetings we helped ourselves to the use of this luxurious setting. While we were seated in that spectacle of splendour we felt as though we were the lords and ladies of the realm. We certainly had a unique setting for our staff meetings.

One evening, however, this room proved to be a stumbling-block. That was the night when we had our first parent-teacher interviews at that school. As I drove into the school parking lot well before the interviews started I was surprised to see an abundance of cars there, and when I checked up inside the building I found that there was a special, hastily-planned meeting going on in the board room. Our school had not been informed of this meeting.

Our interviews proceeded as planned, with the caretaker ringing the bell every ten minutes to announce that time was up for that interview. After the first two interviews, however, the director of education appeared at the office to say that the bells were interrupting an important meeting going on in the board room, and that he would appreciate it if our interviews could carry on without the bell being rung.

Naturally we obliged him. Word was quickly spread to the seven teachers concerned that the interviews would continue as usual but from then on the bell would not ring to signal the end of each one. Each teacher would now have to keep an eye on the clock to make sure every appointed interview began on time – not an easy task to accomplish.

Somehow we managed, but it must have been quite a trial for three members of the staff who were new to the teaching profession. That night our "gift" reminded me a bit of the story of the Trojan horse.

25. For Whom Are You Working?

Ask children in the primary grades this question and they will answer "for the teacher". Ask the same question to university or college students and they will surely reply "for ourselves". Now where along the road of education does this transition take place? Although it's probably a gradual conversion I would hope from my experience as a teacher that it would occur by the latter years of elementary school.

Proof that youngsters have made this change is when, after finishing an assignment well ahead of others in class, they find something worthwhile to do on their own. There is a definite carry-over in this regard when young people leave schooling behind and enter the work force. Different employers I have talked with tell me that they expect their employees to find work to do on their own after they have finished a given task. In other words, no lingering at the water cooler!

I printed this question in the title on a sheet of Bristol board and posted it in a conspicuous place in the classroom. Occasionally I moved it around to give it fresh emphasis. When I found an advantageous situation for it I would interrupt what we were doing and touch it with a pointer to make a point.

There are ways that a teacher can help pupils see they should keep busy on their own when assigned work is finished. I think I shocked some pupils into realizing this whenever I said, "I hope all of you are learning to work for yourselves. I still get paid even if you don't learn what I am teaching you. The big question is, are you using your time wisely to earn your daily pay?"

Here are some things pupils can do profitably in their "spare time." Even with only a few moments available some of my pupils liked looking up meanings of words in a dictionary. This can start what should become a lifelong habit, because the dictionary is one of the few books that should be used throughout one's life. Most classes have a few pupils who show a keen interest in the content subjects – history, geography, science. I've had some pupils who pored over atlases locating the world's longest rivers, largest lakes, and highest mountains. Finally, no children can ever say they have nothing to do if they have a good library book in their desks, something I always insisted upon.

As a teacher I was a great believer in what one man well up the educational ladder in our system said, "If you have nothing to do, don't do it here."